Morning and Evening Meditations
101 Power Thoughts
Overcoming Fears
The Power Is Within You (audio book)
The Power of Your Spoken Word
Receiving Prosperity
Self-Esteem Affirmations (subliminal)
Self-Healing
Stress-Free (subliminal)
Totality of Possibilities
What I Believe and Deep Relaxation
You Can Heal Your Life (audio book)
You Can Heal Your Life Study Course
Your Thoughts Create Your Life

DVDs

Receiving Prosperity
You Can Heal Your Life Study Course
You Can Heal Your Life, THE MOVIE (also available
in an expanded edition)
You Can Trust Your Life (with Cheryl Richardson)

CARD DECKS

Healthy Body Cards
I Can Do It® Cards
*I Can Do It® Cards . . . for Creativity, Forgiveness,
Health, Job Success, Wealth, Romance*
Power Thought Cards
Power Thoughts for Teens
Power Thought Sticky Cards
Wisdom Cards

CALENDAR

I Can Do It® Calendar (for each individual year)

and

THE LOUISE L. HAY BOOK COLLECTION
(comprising the gift versions of *Meditations to Heal Your Life,
You Can Heal Your Life* and *You Can Heal Your Life Companion Book*)

All of the above are available at your local
bookstore, or may be ordered by visiting:

Hay House USA: www.hayhouse.com®; Hay House UK: www.hayhouse.
co.uk; Hay House Australia: www.hayhouse.com.au; Hay House South
Africa: www.hayhouse.co.za; Hay House India: www.hayhouse.co.in

Louise's Websites: www.LouiseHay.com® and www.HealYourLife.com®

ALSO BY DAVID KESSLER

On Grief and Grieving: Finding the Meaning of Grief
Through the Five Stages of Loss
(with Elisabeth Kübler-Ross)

Life Lessons: Two Experts on Death and
Dying Teach Us About the Mysteries of Life and Living
(with Elisabeth Kübler-Ross)

The Needs of the Dying: A Guide for Bringing Hope,
Comfort, and Love to Life's Final Chapter

Visions, Trips and Crowded Rooms:
Who and What You See Before You Die*

* Available from Hay House

Please visit:

Hay House UK: www.hayhouse.co.uk
Hay House USA: www.hayhouse.com
Hay House Australia: www.hayhouse.com.au
Hay House South Africa: www.hayhouse.co.za
Hay House India: www.hayhouse.co.in

❧ ❧ ❧

YOU CAN HEAL *your* HEART

*Finding Peace After a Breakup,
Divorce or Death*

LOUISE L. HAY & DAVID KESSLER

HAY HOUSE

Carlsbad, California • New York City • London • Sydney
Johannesburg • Vancouver • Hong Kong • New Delhi

First published and distributed in the United Kingdom by:
Hay House UK Ltd, Astley House, 33 Notting Hill Gate, London W11 3JQ
Tel: +44 (0)20 3675 2450; Fax: +44 (0)20 3675 2451
www.hayhouse.co.uk

Published and distributed in the United States of America by:
Hay House Inc., PO Box 5100, Carlsbad, CA 92018-5100
Tel: (1) 760 431 7695 or (800) 654 5126
Fax: (1) 760 431 6948 or (800) 650 5115
www.hayhouse.com

Published and distributed in Australia by:
Hay House Australia Ltd, 18/36 Ralph St, Alexandria NSW 2015
Tel: (61) 2 9669 4299; Fax: (61) 2 9669 4144
www.hayhouse.com.au

Published and distributed in the Republic of South Africa by:
Hay House SA (Pty) Ltd, PO Box 990, Witkoppen 2068
Tel/Fax: (27) 11 467 8904
www.hayhouse.co.za

Published and distributed in India by:
Hay House Publishers India, Muskaan Complex, Plot No.3, B-2,
Vasant Kunj, New Delhi 110 070
Tel: (91) 11 4176 1620; Fax: (91) 11 4176 1630
www.hayhouse.co.in

Distributed in Canada by:
Raincoast, 9050 Shaughnessy St, Vancouver BC V6P 6E5
Tel: (1) 604 323 7100; Fax: (1) 604 323 2600

Cover design: Amy Rose Grigoriou • *Interior design:* Riann Bender

A catalogue record for this book is available from the British Library.

ISBN: 978-1-78180-244-1

Printed and bound in Great Britain by TJ International Ltd, Padstow, Cornwall

CONTENTS

AUTHORS' NOTE

We wrote this book to explore how we grieve and find healing after enduring any type of loss, such as a break-up, divorce, or death. Grieving is challenging, but it is our thoughts that often add suffering to our pain. We hope that this book will expand your awareness and thinking around loss to include love and understanding. Our intention is for you to feel your grief fully without getting stuck in the sorrow and suffering.

Grief is not a condition to be cured but a natural part of life. Spirit does not know loss; it knows that every story begins and every story ends, yet love is eternal. Our hope is that the words on these pages offer you comfort and peace throughout your journey. No book, however, should be used to replace professional help if that is needed. We wish you much love and healing.

— Louise and David

PREFACE

by David Kessler

I've been working in the field of grief for most of my life. I've been fortunate to write four books on the subject, including two with the legendary Elisabeth Kübler-Ross, the renowned psychiatrist and author of the groundbreaking book *On Death and Dying.* During my lectures, I'm continually asked, "Does this grief work apply to divorce?" Even at parties, the newly single person will find me and ask, "Can you help me? I've just gone through a breakup and heard you know a lot about grief."

It's always a reminder that the work I do applies to the ending of relationships and marriages as well as the end of life. The truth is that loss is loss and grief is grief, no matter what it's about or what caused it. I can't count the times I've heard people talk harshly about themselves during a breakup or when a marriage has ended, and I've often thought back to my friend Louise Hay, author of the international bestseller *You Can Heal Your Life,* who always says, "Pay attention to your thinking."

❧ ❧ ❧

In order to launch my latest book, *Visions, Trips, and Crowded Rooms,* I was invited to speak at a Hay House conference. Although my book was being released by Louise's publishing company, I hadn't seen her in years, and I was looking forward to spending some time with her. We'd planned to have lunch right after my presentation.

A few minutes after I'd begun, I could feel something happen in the audience, and I noticed people turning to one another and whispering. I had no idea what was going on, so I just continued speaking. Then it hit me: Louise had walked in and sat down. Despite her efforts to be unnoticed, she just carries that kind of energetic force with her.

At lunch, she and I caught up on mutual friends and what was new, and then she said, "David, I've been thinking about it, and I want you to be with me when I die."

"I would be honored," I replied immediately. Since I am a death and grief expert, it's not unusual for me to get asked things like that. Most people don't want to die alone; they want to know that their lives and deaths will be witnessed by someone who is comfortable with the end of life. To that end, the acclaimed actor Anthony Perkins asked me to be with him when he died. Best-selling author Marianne Williamson asked me to be with her and her father when he passed. And I was there when my mentor Elisabeth Kübler-Ross took her last breath.

Then I asked, "Is there anything going on? Something about your health that I should know about?"

"No," she replied. "I'm 82, healthy as I can be, and I'm living my life fully. I just want to make sure that when the time comes, I live my dying fully."

That is Louise.

During the conference, she was scheduled to screen a documentary called *Doors Opening,* which told the story of her famous Hayrides, weekly Wednesday night meetings for people with AIDS and their loved ones in the 1980s. This was where Louise Hay's world and mine first came together. On the rare occasion that she missed a Wednesday night, I'd fill in for her. And what a thrilling ride it was!

Picture 350 or so attendees, mostly men (and some women) with AIDS. Those were the early days of the epidemic, before treatments became available. For the most part, these people were dealing with a catastrophic event in their lives. And there was Louise, sitting in the midst of it all, not seeing it as catastrophic, but as a life-changing opportunity. During the meetings, she invited a healing energy into the room. Yet she also made it perfectly clear that this was not a pity party—there was no room to be a victim. Rather, these meetings provided a chance to achieve deeper healing: a healing of the soul.

My mind flooded with memories as I recalled those inspiring, magical evenings. Now, more than 25 years later, Louise and I were once again in a room together, reflecting on those days and the profound impact it had on our lives. When the documentary began, after a brief introduction, Louise grabbed my hand, and we started to walk down the aisle. Our plan was to talk and catch up more and then return when the film was over to conduct a question-and-answer session with the audience. We were halfway to the door when she paused.

"Oh, look," Louise said. "There's Tom on the screen." Tom was an original Hayride member who had long since died.

"Everyone is so young," I said.

"Let's sit for a couple of minutes," she whispered as she pulled me into the back row.

We ended up watching the whole documentary. Afterward we got up, composed ourselves, walked onto the stage, and the questions began: "What is sickness?" "If thoughts can create healing, why do we take medicine?" "Why do we die?" "What *is* death?"

Every answer that Louise provided gave information and insight into what illnesses are. Then she would give me a nod to interject my thoughts, as if we were playing tennis and she was volleying the ball to me. Our 10-minute Q&A lasted 45 minutes and probably could have gone on for another few hours. And just when I thought the talk was over, Louise proudly announced to everyone, "Oh, I've arranged for David Kessler to be with me when I die." The audience applauded. What I thought had been a private request, Louise was now sharing with the world. That was an example of her power, honesty, and openness.

That evening, Reid Tracy, the president and CEO of Hay House, told me, "Louise and I were talking about the two of you doing something together. You share a common history and can offer a lot of wisdom. We think you should write a book together." I could only imagine Louise Hay sharing her insights on healing regarding one of life's greatest challenges—whether it's coming to terms with the end of a relationship through divorce or a breakup, facing the death of a loved one, or enduring the many other types of loss, such as the loss of a beloved pet or even a beloved job. Louise's wise words, *Pay attention to your thinking,* flashed through my mind once again. What if she and

I wrote a book together that incorporated her affirmations and knowledge about how our thinking can heal ourselves, with my years of experience in helping others cope with grief and loss?

I thought about how many people a book like this could help. I also thought about what it would be like to work so closely with Louise on such an important topic. It turns out that our collaboration on this book was as seamless as our Q&A session at the conference—adding our own insights picked up over the years while also completing and complementing each other's thoughts on various subjects*.

And so our journey together began.

~

---

* Please note that aside from this Preface and Chapter 1, where I describe the start of our writing process together and share our initial conversations, the voice throughout this book belongs to both Louise and me.

INTRODUCTION

A broken heart is also an open heart. Whatever the circumstances, when you love someone and your time together ends, you will naturally feel pain. The pain of losing a person you love is part of life, part of this journey, but suffering doesn't have to be. Although it's natural to forget your power after you lose a loved one, the truth is that after a breakup, divorce, or death, there remains an ability within you to create a new reality.

Let's be clear here: We're asking you to change your thinking after a loss occurs—not to avoid the pain of grief, but to keep moving through it. We want your thoughts to live in a place where you remember your loved one only with love, not with sadness or regret. Even after the worst breakup, the meanest divorce, and the most tragic death, it *is* possible to achieve this over time. That doesn't mean that you deny or run away from the pain. Instead, you let yourself experience it and then allow a new life to unfold—one where you hold the love dear, not the sorrow.

Here's where our real work begins. There are three main areas we'll be focusing on throughout this book:

1. Helping You Feel Your Feelings

If you're reading this book, then you're most likely hurting—and that's something we don't wish to take away from you. But this time can be a vital window, not only to heal your pain, but, if you feel each of your feelings fully, to also begin to release it. One of the biggest problems is that you might try to push aside or ignore your feelings. You judge them as wrong, too little, or too much. You carry a lot of bottled-up emotions, and anger is often one that is suppressed. In order for it to heal, however, it must be released.

We're not speaking only about anger associated with death, but about anytime we feel anger. Elisabeth Kübler-Ross, the renowned grief expert who identified the Five Stages of Grief, said that we could feel anger, let it pass through us, and be done with it in a few minutes. She went on to say that any anger we feel over 15 minutes is old anger.

Of course anger is only one of the emotions that arise. When a relationship ends, when divorce happens, and even when a death occurs, we are left with so many feelings. Feeling them is the first step toward healing.

2. Allowing Old Wounds to Come Up for Healing

Your loss will also be a window into your old wounds, and like it or not, they are going to come forth. Some of them you may not be aware of. When you're going through a breakup, for example, you may think, *I knew he wasn't going to stay.* In a divorce, you may believe that *I don't deserve love,* or when a loved one dies that, *Bad things always happen to me.* These are negative thoughts that stretch beyond the current loss.

It's certainly helpful to take advantage of grief as a time to reflect on the past with tenderness—but to relive it over and over is painful and nonproductive. That's what you tend to do when you just go back without an intention of healing.

Where did these negative thoughts originate? The answer is that they originated in the past and weren't healed with love. Together we'll shine a light on those old wounds and negative thought processes and begin the healing process with love and compassion.

3. Changing Distorted Thinking about Relationships, Love, and Life

When you grieve any loss, you apply your current thinking, which, at its best, is often distorted. What do we mean by that? It is when your beliefs are colored by the wounds of childhood and shaped by hurts from past relationships. Distorted thinking is often molded by your parents and others in your life who did the best they could, but also carried their own distorted thinking from their childhoods. All of this worked together to form the current self-talk in your mind as you think your same old thoughts over and over again. Then you bring this old thinking, the negative self-talk, to your new loss.

This is why human beings so often talk to ourselves without love and tenderness after we've just lost someone we cared for deeply. We blame ourselves, we throw a pity party, and we even feel that we deserve the pain we're now experiencing. How do we break the cycle? Read on to learn about the importance of positive affirmations and their powerful effect on distorted thinking.

The Power of Affirmations to Heal Grief

Affirmations are statements that reinforce a positive or negative belief. We want to raise your awareness of the negative ones you might use and gently invite new, positive ones into your life. In your thinking, you're always affirming something. Unfortunately, when your thinking is distorted, you're usually repeating negative affirmations.

We're going to lovingly introduce positive affirmations to your grief and your life. These positive statements may feel untrue when you first use them. Let them in anyway. You may be afraid that we're trying to take away your grief or diminish it in some way, but that couldn't be further from the truth. Your grief is yours to feel, but positive affirmations can take away your suffering as well as heal some of your old pain and negative thought patterns. Your negative affirmations are untrue, yet you have no trouble feeling those. Many people unconsciously repeat negative affirmations, being so cruel to themselves when they're hurting. One of the main goals we hope to accomplish in this book is finding a way to change that repetitive negative thinking for good.

As you read the positive affirmations in the upcoming chapters, be sure to apply them to your own experiences. Apply them to your thought patterns—your beliefs, how you view the world—using them to undo your limited, negative thinking. Some affirmations may resolve your old wounds from the past to help you process your current ones so that you can finally fully heal with love.

The Gift of Life after Loss

We're sure you know how to end a relationship. You know how to end a marriage. You even know how to end a life. But do you know how to complete a relationship or a marriage? Do you know how to complete a life? This is another aspect we hope to teach you as we journey together. There are unexpected gifts to be found in life after loss.

These may seem like new concepts to you, but the truth is that not all relationships are meant to last. Some will last a month, others a year, some a decade. You'll feel pain when you believe the one-year relationship should have lasted five years. You feel pain because you think the 10-year relationship should have lasted 25 years. The same is true of marriages. Can you think of a marriage as a success when it ends in divorce? Well, it can be. It can be perfect for the experience that you and your spouse needed.

Even when life ends, there is a rhythm. It is sad, of course, because you want more time with your loved one—that's only natural. But there are only two requirements for a complete life: a birth day and a death day. That's it. We all arrive in the middle of the movie, and we leave in the middle of it. We want to hold on to the connection to our loved one who died; we want to keep our memories . . . and we can eventually release the pain.

We'll get started by examining our thoughts around loss in Chapter 1. What are your thoughts about break-ups? How do you feel about marriages ending? How do you respond when a loved one dies? As we take you through these questions, we'll help you begin to change your thoughts about loss.

In Chapter 2, we move on to relationships. Even though you may be reading this book in the midst of a breakup, others may be in the throes of a divorce or a death. Regardless of your current situation, we encourage you to read this chapter because every marriage and every divorce started with a relationship. Every death is also about a relationship.

Chapter 3 focuses specifically on the grief of a divorce. And then, in Chapter 4, we'll look at grief after a loved one dies. In the same way we suggested that you read the relationship chapter, we also suggest that you read the chapter on death, because every breakup and every divorce is also a death on a certain level.

In the remaining chapters, we'll spend time exploring the many other types of losses that we experience in our lifetime, from the loss of a pet, to the loss of a job, to the loss of a pregnancy, and much more. We'll even examine ways of healing the types of losses that aren't so easily seen on the surface, such as grieving something in life that never was and never will be.

The following pages contain new thinking, heart-warming stories, and powerful affirmations geared to specific situations. The stories throughout are taken from real people in real situations who have lovingly chosen to share their life challenges and lessons with us so that we could share them with you.

Our ultimate wish is for you to discover that no matter what you're facing, you *can* heal your heart. You deserve a loving, peaceful life. Let's begin this healing process together.

— **Louise and David**

∽

CHAPTER ONE

CHANGING OUR THOUGHTS ABOUT LOSS

On my drive to San Diego for my first work meeting with Louise, I thought about what questions I would ask. Louise is known for saying, "Thoughts create." How would that apply in loss? I thought about the breakup of a relationship. I also thought about loss in death, recalling a dear friend who was grieving the sudden, unexpected passing of her husband. I wanted to hear Louise's opinion on this situation. After all, she is practically the mother of the New Thought movement.

A pioneer in mind-body healing, Louise Hay was one of the first to introduce the connection between physical ailments and their corresponding thought patterns and emotional issues. Now I would be asking her to bring her wisdom, experiences, and insights to this most challenging time in a person's life. Even though I had already written four books on the subject myself, I forever remain a student. I mean, honestly, how could anyone say they know *everything* about loss?

Louise herself has written so many books and so many meditations that I was eagerly anticipating her unique perspective on this important topic. Soon after I rang the doorbell to Louise's condo, there she was with her ever-endearing hug, inviting me into her home. She showed me around as I admired her surroundings. I immediately felt that this wonderful home with its plush furniture and myriad mementos she'd collected from her extensive travels to remote parts of the world was befitting a woman of Louise's stature.

I was gazing out at the stunning views from her windows when she turned to me and said, "Shall we talk over lunch? There's a great place around the corner."

Within moments, I was walking arm in arm down the streets of San Diego with Louise Hay. No one would have ever guessed that we were about to discuss one of the most painful subjects in the world as we ate. When we sat, I saw the waitstaff's faces light up at Louise's presence. "You're going to love the food here," she assured me.

After we placed our order, I took out my recorder. "Louise," I said, "I've written so much about the medical, psychological, and emotional aspects of loss and grief. I've also touched on the spiritual aspects in each of my books. While I was at a bookstore the other day, I thought about *this* book and realized that it would be one of the few that is devoted to deeply exploring the spiritual side of relationships ending, divorce, death, and other losses. So tell me your beginning thoughts on these spiritual aspects."

"Our thinking creates our experiences," she began. "That doesn't mean the loss didn't happen or that the grief isn't real. It means that our thinking shapes our experience of the loss."

She continued, "David, since you say we each experience grief differently, let's explore why."

I told Louise about my friend whose husband had died suddenly from a brain bleed. But Louise surprised me when she didn't ask about the nature of my friend's loss. Instead, she said, "Tell me about her thinking. We each feel differently because we have different thoughts about our grief. Her thinking is the key."

I caught myself wanting to ask, "How would *I* know what she was thinking?" But then I realized where Louise was going. "Oh," I said, "her words, her actions, and her grief would reflect her thoughts."

Louise put her hand on mine and smiled. "Yes!" she replied. "Tell me some of the things she says."

"Okay. Some of the things I've heard are: 'I can't believe this is happening,' 'This is the worst thing that has ever happened,' and 'I will never love again.'"

"Good," Louise said. "She's telling us a lot. Let's just take a statement like 'I will never love again.' You know how important I believe affirmations are. Affirmations are positive self-talk, so think about what she's saying to herself in grief. *I will never love again.* That statement can create reality. But more important, it doesn't serve her or her loss. The pain of grief is one thing. Our thoughts then add to the suffering. Out of her pain she may feel like she will never love again. But if she was open to some other ways, some suggestions, she could delve into the underlying beliefs about her statement. Some other thoughts could be:

I have experienced a powerful love in my life.

*This love I feel for my husband is clearly
showing me that it's everlasting.*

*I am reminded of my love for him,
and my heart continues to sing."*

I added, "For people who want to go deeper quicker or have moved further in time away from the death, they might say:

I am open to loving again.

*I am willing to experience love in all
of its forms while I'm still alive."*

Louise leaned in and said, "I hope you realize that we don't say these things only after the death of a loved one. We say these things in our relationship breakups and divorce, too. So let's make sure we examine all of those areas."

❦ ❦ ❦

As Louise and I talked, I thought about how there are people who always take the negative path, yet there are also those who do their best to end things well in relationships and find the positive. Take, for example, Darren and Jessica. Darren saw religion as something for his parents and his family, not something that he had chosen for himself. But then he and Jessica discovered religious science and began attending a local church.

"The sermons covered familiar, everyday topics," Darren said, "like buying a home, falling in love, getting married, managing money, and much more, but always with no judgments. Only acceptance and wisdom. This spiritual talk was about a far-more expansive love than what Jessica and I were raised with. As the years passed, we would read books, meditate, and go to workshops. The joke was that years later we realized that our adage, 'Karma sees all,' was a lot like our parents' Golden Rule."

After 22 years of what had seemed to him to be a good marriage, Darren felt that something had changed in the relationship. As Jessica explained to me later, "Life seemed half over and yet underexplored fully. I felt it first. I wanted out, I wanted more. It wasn't about sex or affairs. It was just that I had signed up for a lifelong commitment without fully understanding how long life was and how much there was to do. I loved Darren, but he was happy being at home doing nothing and just relaxing. The slower life that suited Darren was boring for me.

"When I told him that I wanted our relationship to end in its current form and I wanted out, he was furious. He felt I had betrayed him. He took it personally, but it wasn't personal. He accused me of not loving him anymore, but that wasn't true. I did still love him, but the reality was that our romantic relationship was over. I knew that if I stayed, both of us would become very unhappy. It was sad, but I had to go."

The truth is that all of us are always moving toward exploring the wounds that need healing. Our progress may not always be obvious or smooth, but love will deliver everything unlike itself to our doorstep for healing. So while Darren perceived heartbreak from the split, his wife felt not fear or hurt but an overwhelming sense of adventure. As she packed her bags, she gently wiped the tears from his face and said, "You think I'm leaving you, but I'm not. I'm moving out, but I'll still be in the world with you. You think I don't love you but I do, and this is what is best for both of us. I know on some level that if it's right for my future, then it must be right for yours."

Darren remained hurt and angry. "Just admit it," he said. "You don't love me anymore."

Jessica replied, "Sometimes saying good-bye is another way of saying I love you."

It was stories like theirs that often didn't get retold in the breakup world. I often ponder how little we know about ending things like relationships, marriages, and jobs. We just don't know how to *complete* them, and it's hard to accept that while every relationship has a beginning, some of them also have endings.

Honoring the Love

Louise and I were deep in discussion about dealing with grief when our food arrived. Smiling, she looked at her meal and smelled it; then she gave thanks, which felt more genuine and deeper to me than the typical grace we utter out of obligation or habit.

"You really meant that, didn't you?" I asked when she was finished praying.

"Yes," she told me, "because life loves me, and I love life. I am so thankful."

I must admit that, at first, this felt a little over the top. But then I remembered whom I was sitting with—the one person who has proven time and again that affirmations work. I'd just been caught off guard as I saw this tool actually playing out in Louise's life. She savored every bite of her lunch as she explained to me that affirmations are not about pretending that grief doesn't exist. "It doesn't go away if you pretend it isn't there. What do you think happens to it?"

"If you're not ready to experience it," I said, "I believe it will remain on hold for you to deal with when you're ready. If not now, then later. The timing is your choice, and there are periods when we need to shelve our grief. It may be too soon, too painful; or maybe you're too busy raising a child or holding on to a job. Whatever your situation, there will come a time when grief has sat too long on the shelf. It will become old, unattended, angry, and will begin to impact your life in a negative way. But that doesn't have to be your reality."

Louise nodded. "You have the power within you to create a new, more positive reality. When you change your thoughts about grief and loss, it doesn't mean you won't feel the pain or you won't go through the grief. It just means that you won't get stuck in any one feeling. When people look back on loss, they often say that they're glad they felt their emotions fully. They're glad they gave themselves time to fully mourn the end of the relationship. Or if a loved one died, they're glad they honored their grief afterward. However, I've frequently heard people say after an extended grieving period that 'I didn't need to give the pain as much time as I did.'"

We then talked about a 29-year-old woman named Caroline who was just getting back into the dating scene. She said she didn't regret any relationship she'd had, but she did regret taking the last five years to get over a three-year relationship.

"I see that," I said. "A woman once shared with me that nearly a decade after her husband had died in an auto accident, she realized that she would miss him and love him for the rest of her life. But she would rather have learned

YOU CAN HEAL YOUR HEART

sooner to remember their love. When she and I were nearly finished working together, she told me, 'Honoring the love—that's what I'm going to do from here on out. No more honoring the pain.'"

"That's what we want to teach. We want to honor the love, not the pain and not the suffering." Louise looked directly into my eyes and continued. "In this book, we'll teach about intentions. The work will be about affirmations applied to grief and loss. It will bring hope to sorrow. We can teach people that they *can* go from grief to peace, and show them how to do it. They can heal their losses and their hearts. It doesn't have to hurt for the rest of their lives, but they aren't going to get there in a day."

"Very true," I replied. "Healing from loss isn't like getting a cold and a week later, you're better. Healing takes time, but we can teach people to say that they're looking forward to peace. The grief before the peace is extremely important because it is an authentic expression of your feelings as you build a new foundation, a stronger one."

❧ ❧ ❧

I often think about Kübler-Ross's Five Stages of Grief: *denial, anger, bargaining, depression,* and *acceptance.* Healing your heart is about ultimately finding acceptance and living in reality. I'm not suggesting you'll be glad that a loss has happened or say that it's okay. But you have to acknowledge the reality of it, even though all you want is your loved one back.

I shared the following story with Louise:

Christina was a young woman who was diagnosed with early-onset ovarian cancer. It was very aggressive, and it seemed like everyone in her life was trying to deal with the news when things shifted to the fact that she was dying. In an unusual twist, sometimes people who are very young find it easier to accept death than their parents do. In Christina's case, it was her mother, Debra, who was struggling to keep up with the events that were happening. Christina was an interesting, brave soul who had an insight into her world about what she could change and what she could not. She knew that she was dying and accepted it, which brought her a certain kind of peace.

During her illness, she and her mother would often argue. Debra would say, "You're just too young to die."

"Well, how do you explain the fact that I'm dying?" was Christina's reply.

"Your life is incomplete; you can't die so young."

"Mom, there are only two requirements for a complete life: birth and death. Soon my life will be complete because I will have lived and I will have died. That's just the way it is, and we have to find peace in it."

If anything kept Christina up at night, it was worrying about her mother. After Christina passed, I would see Debra every few months, and I still think about how Christina wanted peace so much for her mother, and yet it eluded her. But years later, I ran into Debra and immediately sensed a shift that I couldn't explain. I asked her if anything had changed, and she told me, "I admitted that I wanted Christina back more than I wanted peace. Eventually, I realized that I wanted peace for myself and for Christina. I finally understood what it meant to want someone you love to *rest in peace.*"

"To this day," I told Louise, "Christina and Debra always remind me of how important it is to want that peace."

Louise agreed. "We forget to feel and understand the words from our upbringing. Think about those words *rest in peace.* We've all heard them, but in Debra's situation, she ultimately wanted her daughter to find that peace, knowing that love is eternal and never dies. And likewise, Christina would have wanted her mother to rest in peace every night as well, acknowledging the bond that death cannot sever. Now Debra rests in her firm belief that they will one day see each other again."

Whatever kind of loss your grief stems from, it's vital to hold the thought of *wanting* to find peace and to find a healing of the heart. It is comforting and powerful to know that fully grieving and finding peace is always an available option. In fact, this book contains a number of options that you may not have considered before, including challenging your thoughts and using affirmations to change unhealthy thought patterns.

Just remember that healing your loss *and* your heart is possible. People do it successfully all the time, but you must always keep in mind that your grief is as unique as your fingerprint. You must recognize your loss and your grief in order to heal your heart fully. People often get mad at friends who don't understand their loss. They may not and perhaps never will, but only you can truly appreciate your loss because it is you and you alone who can heal it.

Different Kinds of Loss

Most people are surprised to learn that there are many different types of loss. "Loss is loss," they say, and that is true on one level; however, since there are so many kinds of specific losses, it's worth looking at the archetypes.

In the remainder of the chapter, we'll focus on *complicated loss, loss in limbo,* and *disenfranchised grief.* It's important to remember that grief is a reaction to those losses.

While we don't want to dwell in the intricacies of the types, understanding what kind of loss you're experiencing can sometimes help you find your "best self" in the situation.

Complicated Loss

To put it simply, *complicated loss* is any loss that is complicated by other factors. Most of us know that we will experience loss when a relationship naturally ends. When two people mutually agree on separation and divorce, that is an uncomplicated loss. When the death of an elderly relative happens in an expected way after a good, long life, that is an uncomplicated loss. How many of these are there? How often does everyone agree, and how often do things end well?

Everyone's lives are complicated, and so are their losses, of course. Losses become complicated when you don't expect them to happen. In other words, this loss was a surprise. While you may name it, and it may well be a complicated loss, no matter how complex, the possibility for healing is always there. Let's look at some examples of how we can change our thinking.

In a relationship, when one person wants a separation and the other one doesn't, you may want to add this to your thinking:

> *While I don't understand this separation now,*
> *I will accept it as reality so healing can begin.*

This same thinking can be used with divorce:

> *I don't believe we need to divorce, but my husband*
> *wants it [or, my wife has filed the papers]. While*

*I don't agree with it, I do believe that we choose our
own destiny, and my partner has chosen his.*

Everyone has a right to choose to be in a marriage or not.

When someone dies young, you might say to yourself:

*I didn't see this death coming. I believed this person had more
to experience in life, but I remind myself that I do not see all
or know all. While I may have feelings of anger and confusion,
I don't know what anyone's journey is supposed to be.*

Remember that while the loss may be complicated,
the healing doesn't have to be.

Loss in Limbo

Here are some examples of *loss in limbo:* after the third
break in a relationship, a couple might say, "The separation
is killing us. We wish we could make this work or finally end
it for good."
Some helpful affirmations may be:

This separation will reveal helpful information.

This relationship will grow or end in its own time.

Individuals dealing with serious, ongoing health-care
issues might say, "The days spent waiting for test results
are excruciating," or "I either want to completely get better
or die."
A good affirmation to use may be:

My health is not solely defined by a test result.

Wondering if there is going to be a loss can feel as bad as the loss itself. Life sometimes forces you to live in limbo, not knowing if you will experience loss or not. You may have to wait several hours to hear if your loved one's surgery went well, or days until a loved one is out of a coma. You may wait in limbo for hours, days, weeks, or longer when a child is missing. The families of soldiers who are missing in action are often wrenched by decades of living in limbo. And years later, those left behind still haven't resolved their losses and may not be able to do so until they learn the truth. But that information may never come. Being in the limbo of loss is, in itself, a loss.

It doesn't have to be that way, however. In the storm, you can find a port. During the limbo of loss, you'll probably scare yourself with the worst possible outcomes. You don't know how you'll survive if this loss actually happens. In these situations, you can become paralyzed and are no help at all to others or yourself. A healing affirmation for this situation is:

> *Even though I do not know the whereabouts of*
> *my loved one, I trust that he or she is safely cared*
> *for in the loving hand of God.*

In a breakup, for example, you might think, *I must get him back; I'm not ready for this to end.* Well, think again! What if instead you said to yourself:

> *I may not know the outcome, but life loves me,*
> *and I will be fine with him or without him.*

If you're having a hard time breaking up with someone, try saying this to yourself:

If I am not the one for her, someone else is!
Let me get out of the way so that they can come together.

Disenfranchised Grief

Disenfranchised grief is the result of a loss for which people do not feel they have a socially recognized right to grieve. Disenfranchised grief is often not openly mourned or approved of. Some examples are:

- The relationship is not socially approved of or publicly recognized, such as a gay or lesbian relationship or marriage.
  Try thinking:

  Regardless of what others think about my love,
  I honor my love and my loss.

- The relationship exists primarily in the past: for example, the deceased is an ex-wife or ex-husband.
  Try thinking:

  Even though my loved one is my ex, my feelings
  of love are not just in the past, but also in the present.
  I will fully grieve my love for him or her.

- The loss is hidden or not easy to see. Hidden losses include abortion or miscarriages.
  Try thinking:

  I see and honor the loss of my child.

- There is a stigma connected to how the person died. This could be a death that appears to have an element of poor decision making or what some consider sin. Suicide, AIDS, alcoholism, or drug overdose are all examples.
  Try thinking:

For suicide: *My loved one was in pain and could not see a way out. I now see him as whole and at peace.*

For AIDS: *My loved one is beautiful and worthy, regardless of her illness.*

For alcoholism and/or drug addiction: *My loved one did the best he could. I remember him before he was addicted, and I see him now without his addiction.*

- The loss of a pet sometimes isn't shared because of the fear of ridicule.
  Try thinking:

  The love I have for my pet is very real.
  I will only share my grief with those
  who will understand my loss.

Remember, when it comes to disenfranchised grief, you can't change other people's thinking, but you can always change your own.

I honor my losses.

❧ ❧ ❧

As you see, there are different names for different types of losses. While each one of us grieves in a unique way, the experience of loss is universal. It is important to note then, that if loss is universal, so is healing. While you often have no control over a breakup, divorce, or death occurring, you do have complete control over the thinking that follows. You can create an experience of fully feeling the grief and desiring the healing, or you can become a victim of the pain. Affirmations are a valuable tool that can steer your thoughts toward healing and away from suffering.

Let's now take a closer look at loss through a breakup in a relationship and learn how to focus our thoughts on healing, as well as ways to break through negative beliefs so that we can manifest greater love for ourselves in the future.

~

CHAPTER TWO

BREAKUPS AND BREAKTHROUGHS IN **RELATIONSHIPS**

The words people say to themselves and the words heard after a breakup have an impact and a message. Folks know that the messages in fairy tales are not the truth. When we hear, "and then they lived happily ever after," we all know there is no real happily ever after. Maybe there is an "authentically ever after," a "hope-fully ever after," or even a "perfect-for-us ever after."

Wouldn't it be great if after a relationship, you could just shake hands with the person and say, "Thanks, that was great," and then go on your way? Or perhaps, "Thanks, I learned a lot of lessons out of that," or "What a wild ride that was! Take care."

However, most of the time you are in deep grief and feel as if you're standing under a dark cloud. Are there other options that you might think and perceive? The grief is real, but does there have to be a dark cloud? Could you be in the afterglow of love instead? Could you surround yourself in the gratitude of your love? Could you stop and think, *Wow, what an interesting time in my life that was. Wasn't that an amazing chapter?* Could you be curious about what's coming next? Do you really have to be stuck under the dark cloud, waiting for the storm to come?

Like most human beings, you probably see being in love as a hill with no relationship to the valley. Do the times when you're alone have value? We hope you will allow yourself to feel the pain of grief after a relationship ends, but know that constant negative thoughts will only add to the suffering.

Talk to people, especially older people. Hear how amazing their lives were when they were in relationships *and* when they were without a relationship. In all levels of consciousness, speaking, meditating, praying, and saying affirmations have tremendous healing power. And so does silence. Some will even tell you that when their relationship ended, it was a profound time in their lives, a time of re-creation, reformation, and growth.

In this chapter, we'll share many powerful stories and insights on breaking through after a relationship ends. If you can, try to open your mind to seeing how the end of a relationship can be perceived differently, even in a positive light. Part of what keeps many tormented is fear, and one of the underlying fears in the loss of a relationship is abandonment. For example, you might think, *He was supposed to be with me.* How do you know that for sure? Maybe that simply isn't true, but there are other ways to see it. Perhaps you were supposed to be with this person in a romantic relationship from age 23 to 25, and then you were supposed to be with someone else from age 30 to 51. People come in and out of your life, but love doesn't have to.

Once again, this may sound like we're asking you to change your thinking, and we are. But what limits your thinking is when you believe that you only have *one way* of thinking in loss—usually a negative one. Ultimately, you really want to expand your thinking so that you see many options and unlimited ways to perceive the events in your life.

Relationships offer us all new opportunities to understand who we are, what we fear, where our power comes from, and what the meaning of true love is. The idea that relationships are learning opportunities may seem counterintuitive because we know that they can be frustrating, challenging, even heartbreaking experiences. And yet they can be so much more. Relationships give us our greatest chance to find real love and true healing.

When you're grieving after a breakup, you can wrongly perceive that your wholeness has vanished. When you think your wholeness is impacted by someone else, you believe that you yourself are not enough—you're not complete, you can't find your own love, and you can't create your own happiness in your personal and work lives. Instead of trying to find the right person to love, let's make *you* more worthy of being loved. Rather than constantly asking your current partner to love you more, become more worthy of being loved by them. And if you are worthy and they still leave, then they weren't the right one for you.

To find love, you must ask yourself if you're giving as much love as you wish to get, or if you expect people to love you more than you love them or yourself. The old saying rings true: "If your boat doesn't float, no one will want to sail across the ocean with you."

Seeing Relationships Differently

Before we examine the grief of relationships, we must look at how people think when they're in them.

However you think in the midst of a relationship is how you will grieve afterward. For instance, if you were coming from lack in the relationship, your grief will also reflect lack. If you were full of anger in the relationship, you will also have anger along with grief after that relationship. The truth is that we don't just want to introduce a more expanded way of thinking about grief after a relationship. We want you to also see how expanded thinking might work *during* a relationship.

Joanna and her identical twin, Grace, were born minutes apart, but by chance Joanna was born two minutes before midnight on New Year's Eve, and Grace was born shortly after that. Even though one sister was only minutes older than the other, they proclaimed their different birthdays proudly. And these identical twins were also very different in how they managed relationships.

Grace was seeing a computer specialist who developed software to oversee how prescribed medications would interact with each other. He was considered a hero by many since his work saved lives. Grace enjoyed being with him and loved their relationship, so when he announced to her one day that he had met someone else, she was devastated. She would say things like, "I guess that wasn't meant to be. Ultimately, that wasn't the right relationship for me." She had a unique way of seeing things for what they were. "I guess that relationship was only meant to last a year," she remarked.

Her twin sister asked her, "Didn't you think he was the one?"

Grace answered, "Well, if he was the one, we'd still be together. The fact that the relationship is over means that it was supposed to be for a year, not a lifetime."

Joanna painfully looked on, but her pain was not limited to her view of her sister's relationship. Her pain clearly shaped her own experience of love and romance, which had only two states: she was either in a relationship or she was in regret about a relationship. Her primary relationship was with Phil, a handsome sportscaster. In many ways they were a great couple, but she still regretted ending her prior relationship with Max. *If I hadn't made the mistakes I did with Max,* she often wondered, *would we still be together?* When Joanna thought about her current relationship, she was terribly worried about making the same mistakes with Phil.

Grace would simply say, "You need to forget your last relationship and the one before it. You already learned whatever you needed to know. Just be in your current relationship. Be with Phil."

That was easier said than done for Joanna, however. "But what if I'm too quiet or too aggressive?"

"What if, what if . . . what if our grandmother had wheels?" countered Grace. "Would we be cars?"

These sisters were clearly processing relationships, the loss of relationships, and transitions to new ones very differently. But they also experienced individual lessons because even twins are not here to go on each other's journeys. We each have an individualized "flight plan" for our learning. We often try to engineer or diagnose our internal processes and change our lessons, but life is expertly giving us what we need at any given moment.

That doesn't mean we don't live life and experience mistakes. We don't want to take ourselves out of the game of life and just examine it. There is a point where self-examination becomes self-indulgence, and we must move on in order to change. We can't control others, we can't change our past, but we have full control over our inner dialogue. Once Joanna realizes that her negative thoughts interfere in her relationships, then and only then will she gain the self-awareness that her thoughts can create a different reality.

Consider a thought such as, *I know I'm going to make the same mistake again.* We cannot only change it, but we can also use it as a guide for our healing. It could literally turn into a meditation with a mantra such as:

I have healed from my past mistakes.

Joanna was able to move past her mistakes in her last relationship. People sometimes think, *Great, I've healed. Now everything will be perfect.* The truth, however, is that the world always moves toward healing, so for Joanna, it will not necessarily be smooth sailing. But in time, she will move on to her next area of healing.

When you heal part of yourself, the Universe does not say, "Let's give her six months of smooth sailing." The Universe says, "What is the next thing about Joanna that needs healing to move her toward happiness?" Many spiritual paths include the concept that anything unlike love will be brought up for healing. In Joanna's case, she looked at another personality trait that did not serve her. She began a diagnostic panel of Phil, asking herself: *Is he the one for the rest of my life? Would he be a good father? Will the sex always be good? Do my friends like him? Will my family approve?*

You may think that these sound like reasonable questions to ask, and they are. But not a hundred times a day. Many people aren't aware that they have 70,000 thoughts per day, and the shocking news is that these thoughts are mostly repetitive. Joanna's concept of a life or a relationship that is too closely examined is a life or a relationship that is not truly lived. You can't be present in the moment—genuinely honest and open—if you're too busy running an analysis.

Let's go back and examine some more of Joanna's thoughts in her relationship that impact her grief if the relationship ends, as well as the quality of the relationship that she is having now.

Here's the first question she asked: "Is he the one for the rest of my life?"

The true answer to her question is that he's the one for today. There is nothing to question beyond the present moment. There is no happiness to be found in the future. The very fact that he is here today means that he is the one for today.

Can you begin to see that this will help you live in the moment and in reality? "He is the one for today" is truthful. "He is the one for the rest of my life" may or may not be true. You simply can't know whether or not you'll be with someone for the rest of your life. When a relationship ends, you'll feel grief, but it's so much worse if you believe that your partner was "the one," and now you have lost your "forever" mate. Remember to use this affirmation:

He is the one for today.

Let's take a look at Joanna's second question: "Would he be a good father?"

Whenever our thinking is focused on another person rather than ourselves, we won't find happiness. For Joanna, the question should not be whether Phil would be a good father, but rather would she be a good mother when the day arrived. Let's be real here. Can we ever really know whether or not someone else will make a good parent? Many of us have had siblings or friends who we thought would make great parents, but they turned out to lack certain skills. At the same time, we've been surprised by others who we thought would be bad parents, and they turned out to be great ones. In the end, Joanna only has control of her own parenting skills, if and when that day comes. A more positive affirmation for her would be:

I am going to work hard to be the best mother I can be.

Joanna's third question was: "Will the sex always be good?"

Ultimately, sex exists in only one place: between your ears. How turned on you will be in the future is none of your business. How much of yourself you bring to your sexual experience is all you need to focus on. Joanna can bring all her intensity, passion, creativity, excitement, and sense of adventure to her bedroom tonight. A positive affirmation would be:

I will bring all of myself to my sexual experience tonight.

"Do my friends like him?" was Joanna's next question.

Your friends will be a reflection of the thoughts you send out. If you pose a question that contains doubt, they will have doubts. On the other hand, if you send out thoughts of happiness, your friends will automatically like your significant other because they see that you are happy. The positive affirmation is:

My friends will like me being happy in his presence.

And finally, Joanna wondered, "Will my family approve?"

Maybe and maybe not. Most of the time, your family members will pick up on your emotions. If they don't approve, remember that this is your life, this is your relationship. Only one person truly needs to approve of this relationship. *You.* A positive affirmation is:

I approve of my relationship.

All of our thoughts are valuable. You can't think one way during a relationship and then think completely differently in your grief after a breakup. If your thinking during the relationship is negative and distorted, your grief will be negative and distorted. It's vital to see this as a continuum because if you believe that a relationship will go sour, your negative thoughts that permeated the relationship will permeate your grief. And when a new relationship comes along, you won't suddenly have magical, clear thinking. You will be a victim of your patterns.

Grief is the window that provides the opportunity to examine your primal thinking about relationships. If you grieve relationships well, you will relate well. If you relate poorly in the relationship, you have another opportunity to change your thinking in how you grieve and how you handle the next relationship.

Knowing Who You Are

Vanessa laughs when she thinks back to her "dream" relationship. Happily married now to a man who was not the dream, she remembers that first big relationship with humor and love, and no longer with pain.

When she was 27, she was overjoyed when she met Ron, a pediatrician, at a party. She always knew that someday she would meet someone special who would recognize her specialness, too. She wondered what it would be like to be one of those women who married a doctor.

After 11 months of dating, Vanessa felt like she had arrived and grown up when Ron invited her to move in. *It is my destiny to marry a doctor,* she thought to herself. *I'll do charity events for the hospital. When he complains about work, I'll be the one who knows what it took for him to become the doctor that he is. When people talk about how much money he makes, I'll remind them of how much schooling was required to get where he is.*

Vanessa went from hanging out at her local coffeehouse to having tea with the other doctors' wives. And yet, it wasn't all perfect. Ron could be a bit arrogant and self-centered. At one point, she suggested that they redecorate his bedroom, which looked more like a bachelor's pad with its water bed and wet bar. He snapped and said that his room was just fine. He'd had that water bed for more than a decade and loved everything about it, except of course when he had to drain it and refill it with fresh water. He told Vanessa how cold that first night always was when the water had just been changed. So she put changing the bedroom out of her mind for the time being, knowing that eventually she would get the opportunity to redo it.

They celebrated their first anniversary with a trip to Maui, Ron's favorite island. But Vanessa had also allowed a guest to join them—her fear.

When Vanessa asked Ron if he had brought other women there in the past, he said, "Yes. This has always been my favorite place, and I came here with previous girlfriends and also when I was single. I once met someone here who ended up becoming my girlfriend."

His honesty only made Vanessa more insecure, so let's examine her thinking at this point. Her thoughts were: *Am I just a number to him? If I hadn't joined him in Maui, would he have found someone else to keep him company? Will he ever marry me?*

You might imagine her bottom-line question to be: *Do I really matter? Does he love me?* But that wasn't the issue here; it wasn't one particular thought. Rather, it was that all of her insecure thoughts boiled down to: *I'm invisible. I'm not worth it. I am completely replaceable.*

If you focus on the negative like Vanessa did, life gets worse, but if you focus on the positive, life gets better. While Ron may have been arrogant, what thoughts did he pick up from Vanessa? She felt unlovable, unworthy, and invisible. What was there for him to love? Or the more precise questions are: Who was there for him to love? If Vanessa wasn't enough for herself, how could she be enough for him?

We wish we could tell you that Ron and Vanessa had a wonderful time in Maui, but in reality, she became her insecurities. And he became even more aloof. When they returned from their trip, he'd hoped that life would get back to normal, but Vanessa's insecure thoughts continued to plague her. *I bet other women have lived in this house,* she kept telling herself. She repeated that thought so often that it eventually demanded an answer. So she curtly asked him, "Have other women lived in this house with you?"

Once again, Ron answered honestly, "Yes, but what difference does it make? You're here now."

"I just needed to know," she said. But in a few days, she asked, "Did they break up with you, or did you break up with them?" She had taken her focus off of *being in* the relationship and put it on the *end of* the relationship. She wasn't living life; she was already in grief.

Ron realized that trying to reassure her would be pointless. He could feel the downward pull of her emptiness and her neediness. Eventually, the negative words that she had been expecting came: "Vanessa, I think you should move out." Her negative affirmations had created her worst fear.

She pleaded with him to change his mind, but his decision had been made. She moved out in a frenzy of rage. She knew she had been right all along. She was just a number, another girlfriend. Nothing more.

For the next few days, Vanessa found herself in a dark place. All of the thoughts and insecurities she had brought into the relationship had shaped her grief. Her negative thoughts continued as she angrily got her stuff out of his place and moved in with Yvonne, an old friend.

After a few days, Yvonne said to her, "Listen to yourself . . . I can understand why he didn't want to be with you. *You* don't want to be with you! You have no self-worth. You describe yourself the way he saw you. Who are you? Do you even know?"

Still trapped in her negative affirmations, Vanessa vowed that she would make Ron miss her, and she knew what she needed to do. She still had a key to his house and knew that Wednesday was always his busiest day in the office. When he was seeing his first patient of the day, she went to his house and let herself in.

She remembered he had complained of the cold the first night after the water bed had been refilled, so she began to drain it. For the next few hours, she sat by the bed, watching the water empty, thinking how alone and cold he would feel that night and then he would want her back. When the water had drained, she began the refilling process. Then she made the bed as if nothing had happened and left.

The next morning, knowing that he must have missed her terribly during the night, she waited by the phone for his call. By 4 P.M., shocked that she hadn't heard from him, she decided to call his office. He took the call, and she asked him how was doing.

"Fine," he replied, sounding distracted.

Frustrated, she asked, "How did you sleep?"

"Fine."

She hung up the phone. She thought about the effort she'd exerted in trying to make him feel uncomfortable and alone. She wanted him to feel the pain of loss that she was feeling. When Yvonne got home, Vanessa told her what she had done.

"Vanessa," her friend said, "look where your thinking has gotten you. You're conspiring with his water bed to make him feel like he misses you. But the key is, where are *you* in the situation? What was so great about you that would make him miss you? Where was your laughter, your smile, your great sense of style? Your love of board games? Your warm personality? You made yourself completely invisible and then accused him of not seeing you, or of him seeing you as just another number. Well, now you're Crazy Girl #5 who let the water out of a water bed to make her boyfriend miss her. No one is going to think about *you* and how special you are until you do."

What Yvonne said finally struck a chord in Vanessa, and she focused on her negative thinking for the first time. She knew that her behavior with the water bed was ridiculous, but she hadn't put the threads together. Now she would need to show up for her grief, feel it, and deal with it herself. She finally understood that until she showed up for her life, no one else would.

For the next few years, Vanessa thought about who she was in the world, not in relation to her destiny as a doctor's wife, or anyone else's wife for that matter. She volunteered at charities because she wanted to, and she began to search for her favorite place in the world instead of being fixated on some guy's favorite spot. She started to see her life as a seed that needed nurturing, not as a vine that was growing on someone else's wall. She realized that looking at the other person kept her distracted from the real work in the relationship—*herself.*

After continuing to work on herself for a few years, she met a great guy named Hank, who loved Vanessa for who she was. The water-bed incident became nothing more than a story that got rolled out every few parties by Vanessa or someone else. She often ended the story with: "If you think negative thoughts, you're going to end up wasting a day draining someone else's water bed. When you think good thoughts, you end up happy. And you end up sleeping well, too!"

As the saying goes: *How empty of me to be so full of you.* The only person any of us need to focus on—the only one we can work on—is the one in the mirror. It's always an "inside" job.

In the end, Vanessa realized that her actions hadn't just been about wanting Ron to feel the pain she felt. It was about the abandonment that came up for her around him. Perhaps more important, she was learning how she had abandoned herself. She found that if she allowed herself to grieve, she was able to create a way to examine abandonment, meet it with understanding and love, and ultimately heal it. And that's what grieving well means.

As you begin to see relationships differently, you'll recognize that they have their own rhythmic flow. Some will last a lifetime, others a few decades, some a few years, and some only a few months. But there can be no judgment here. No matter how long you were with a person, the breakup deserves its personal time of grief. Grief after a relationship gives you the opportunity to understand your own healthy and unhealthy archetypes.

Some people are astounded to witness the repetitive negative affirmations they say to themselves after a loss of a relationship, but these can be insightful moments that bring us closer to real love and healing. We see, perhaps for the first time, that how we grieve a relationship reveals how we acted in that relationship. Ultimately, as soon as we spot those negative affirmations, we can turn them into positive ones that can reshape our future life and loves.

The Wrong Person Can Be the Perfect Person

Many of us think that this relationship went sour or that one was a waste of time, and consider those months or years as something we will never get back. But the truth is that each relationship is an experience that we have been uniquely and personally assigned, whether we are with that person for a week, a month, or a decade.

When Marissa turned 30, she was still single. She'd had two prior relationships that had left her feeling terribly abandoned, and she decided to get proactive and take matters into her own hands. She joined a popular online dating service and checked in every day to see if someone had "winked," "flirted," or sent her a message.

She made the decision to meet every guy who showed an active interest in her, so she had lunches, dinners, coffees, and drinks. Then when her work sent her to a nearby state for a conference, she found that the man in the seat next to her on the flight home seemed very interested.

He politely introduced himself. "I'm Will."

"My name is Marissa."

For the next hour, they were deep in conversation. Marissa loved his energy, and when the flight attendant announced that the seat-belt sign would be coming on soon, Marissa quickly rushed to the bathroom to freshen up. She looked at her face in the mirror and considered putting on some makeup for him. Then she realized, *Well, he's already seen me without makeup, and he seems to like me.*

When she returned to her seat, Will said, "It would bring great joy to me—and I hope to you, too—if you would join me for dinner."

She smiled and said, "I would never want to deny you the pleasure of bringing great joy into my life."

"How about tomorrow night?"

She loved that he made a plan so quickly. He even chose the time and restaurant.

They went to dinner and chatted like they were old friends. "For our second date," Will asked, "would you be available tomorrow night for dinner?"

She agreed. At the end of the evening, he said, "Obviously, I'd really like to see you again. When are you available?"

Marissa said, "Three nights in a row seems like it would be too much, and we'd be breaking all the dating rules. So let's do it anyway."

The intimacy was great; the company was great; and yes, the sex was great. Marissa had a real sense that this was "the one," the guy she'd been waiting for. On Thursday night, she said, "So what's your weekend like?"

"I do consulting for nonprofit agencies," Will said. "I'm running a board retreat this weekend, but I'll be back late Sunday night."

"Where are you going?" Marissa asked. "Anywhere I can tag along and get a few spa treatments while you're working?"

"This one's tough," Will told her. "I have lots of dinners scheduled and wouldn't get to see you at all."

Marissa felt a horrible pang in her gut, but she tried not to let her feelings show. She wanted to say that they could at least sleep together, but she knew that would be too much.

"I'll call you Monday morning when I get back to town, and we can make plans then," he said.

Marissa was walking on air and thought of nothing but him. She immediately put her membership on hold at the dating service. On Saturday night, she met her closest girlfriends for dinner and told them about Will. One friend said, "Take it slow because you don't really know this guy yet." Another friend said, "Don't see him every night. Don't be so available. Guys like the chase." And the last friend said, "You're all so cynical. Let her enjoy herself and just be real." Marissa just listened and smiled, unfazed. She believed what was going on was good.

On Monday morning, the phone never left her hand. She was a wreck until he finally called at 11:30.

"Are you free anytime soon?" Will asked.

"I think I'm free tonight," she said.

They both laughed. She felt her pain subside since she had been saving this night for him. They had another great evening together, and Marissa felt a sense of love and wholeness when she was with Will that she'd never experienced before. They went on having dates nightly for the entire week. But once again, on Thursday night, he told her he would be away for the weekend: "It's rare that I have two board retreats one weekend after the other, but they tend to do that in the spring."

Once again on Monday morning, Marissa waited for his call. When she hadn't heard from Will by noon, she decided to call him. It went straight to voice mail. She called again at 2 and 4 and left a message, but got no reply. She started to get very worried but kept herself in check. *The retreat must have gone on longer than he expected,* she thought. But when he didn't call on Tuesday, she started to get really frightened. Had something happened to him? Was he okay? Maybe he lost his phone?

Then again, if he did, he could have borrowed someone else's to call her.

By Wednesday, his voice mail simply said: "There is no voice mail available for this number." Marissa was angry. She called one of her girlfriends and explained what had happened.

"Whoa," her friend said, "you need to slow down and get a handle on reality. You just met this guy."

On Thursday night, she had drinks with some other girlfriends, who took her to task on the situation. The first one said, "Have you gone to his house?"

"We'd planned to go sometime soon," Marissa replied, "but he said that a gentleman should always pick up a lady. That's how we always ended up at my place."

"You mean that a *married guy* always picks up a lady at her house."

Marissa was stunned at the accusation. "Will is not married!"

Her friend looked at her for a moment and then said, "Think about it. He's never here on the weekends because he's with his family. He had to disappear because he realized there was nowhere for this to go."

"Maybe he was married," the first friend added, "and he realized that he liked you so much, but he had to end it."

Marissa found no comfort in being with her friends, so she ended the night early, hoping that there was a message from Will on her home phone. But there wasn't.

Over the next week, she expected to eventually hear from him, even if it was to say good-bye. In a few more weeks, her anger had turned to rage at what jerks men could be. She began to doubt her own feelings and felt truly duped. Will had rapidly gone from "He *will* call," to "He *won't* call."

Weeks later, she still found herself calling his cell phone occasionally, but it had been disconnected. She came to the conclusion that he had to be married. Why else would he go so far as to disconnect his cell phone? She couldn't imagine it was some "pay as you go" temporary phone. If it was his real phone, she could have wrecked his marriage with one phone call. Her friends were right, and she had been gullible. She became consumed by the mystery of Will. Did he have a family? What type of person did something like this? What happened to Will and why he did what he did became her obsession. The more she thought about him, the unhappier she became and the more her sense of abandonment grew.

Marissa secluded herself at home, drowning in depression and bitterness. She had never felt so alone. But then after a few weeks, it hit her: *Why am I suffering for five weeks over eight dates in two weeks?* She thanked God it didn't go on for months, or it would have taken her years to recover. She realized that she had given Will more than he deserved, but more important, the degree of pain and grief she felt couldn't possibly be just over this man.

Six weeks later, Marissa signed back on to the dating service, and her friends were happy but encouraged her to take things slow and go easy on herself.

"I've taken six weeks to grieve," Marissa said. "I've felt so alone. I always feel abandoned by guys, but I can't do this anymore. I'm starting to believe that my feelings of loss have very little to do with my dating."

"You don't have to date if you don't want to," one of her friends said.

Marissa shot back, "It's not dating that has to change. It's about always feeling abandoned. In a strange way, dating Will was a great lesson because I was sure he was the one. It made me see what I do, how I set myself up. But I've worked long and hard to change myself and my thinking."

She was referring to the inner work and affirmations she was doing. She realized that every day she had been affirming something. Usually, it was something negative such as, *I feel whole with Will. I need someone to complete me. I am only happy in relationships.*

But now she was counteracting all of that with some new affirmations that she'd learned while working through her deep grief:

I am here for myself.

Men may come and go, but I will
always love and support myself.

We don't know Will's part in this story, but don't doubt that he will learn his lesson also. Since he was hurtful, Marissa could say:

I will not worry because karma sees all.

His journey in life is none of my business.

It might seem strange, but Marissa realized that her brief encounter with Will was a gift. He was the perfect person to help heal her abandonment issues, and in ways that we don't know, she was perfect for him, too.

We could easily just leave it at Marissa met a real jerk, but what would that say about the Universe? It just randomly sent Marissa a thoughtless guy? Why? Just to make her life miserable? Could there be a reason? If this is an all-knowing, all-loving Universe—always moving us toward healing—then there must be a good reason Will was sent to Marissa. Since she was so ready to use this man and the moment in her life to go deeper into her abandonment issues, in many ways the wrong guy was the perfect guy for her healing.

People in intimate relationships usually have the same issues, but in reverse. If you struggle with love, you'll attract someone who has issues with love. If you have issues with power, your partner will, too, although not necessarily in the same way. And then, it may not be that obvious.

If one person is bossy because he fears he lacks power, his partner may be submissive because she fears finding her power. A couple may have problems with addiction, but while one is the addict, the other may be the co-dependent partner or the rescuer. If the shared issue is fear, one partner handles it by being bold and fearless, while the other person is timid and makes little to no decisions. Like often attracts like, but in an "opposite" way. In other words, in any relationship, one person makes pancakes, and the other one eats them.

What that means is that typically, when a problem occurs, one partner wants to talk and work it out, while the other prefers to be quiet, to let things settle down and work themselves out. The more aggressive person pushes all of his buttons, and his "refusal" to deal with it pushes hers. Both people think that the other has a problem and is handling it wrong. But in a very real sense, each one is perfect for the other in that moment, in that relationship.

Aloof and Needy

Another example of a dance we do with each other is known as "Aloof and Needy." While many people deal with abandonment issues, many others are faced with control issues. So it's not surprising to find out that one person experienced abandonment in his or her childhood and the other felt too controlled. When they grow up, one becomes *needy* while the other becomes *aloof,* and it's no surprise that they go on to date each other in adulthood. This may sound extreme, but many of us do have a little bit of both aloof and needy in us.

While the abandoned (needy) individual often fears that the other person will leave, the one with control issues (aloof) fears being overly controlled in the relationship. As the Universe magically brings these two people together to heal each other, the person with the abandonment issue ultimately learns to quit abandoning him- or herself, while the control-issue person needs to feel confident that no one can control him or her.

When people have control issues, they often become aloof and retreat, which of course triggers their partners' abandonment issues. But the truth is they are not being controlled. They are simply a slave to and are being controlled by their own past. When these individuals are in an argument and feel controlled, they are usually living in the past, so in truth they have lost control—not by their partner, but by their past.

Some possible affirmations are:

No one can control me; I am my own master.

*When I am feeling controlled, I release the
past with love and come into the present moment.*

I am free to do whatever I want.

The choice is always mine.

Control-issue people heal by recognizing their freedom and seeing that cause and effect exists in all experiences, but it doesn't originate with their partner. They
have complete freedom to date other people, and the
consequence may be that the relationship doesn't grow.
They may feel that their partner should not expect to be
put first, but the result may be that they are not made a
priority either, which probably doesn't feel very good.

This is true for the abandoned person, too. When
these individuals feel deserted, they reach out to others from their wound, which automatically triggers their
partner's control issues. When they are in their abandonment mode, they are also living in the past. If they
let that run the relationship, no matter what the other
person does, they will automatically feel abandoned.

Some possible affirmations are:

No one can truly abandon me but me.

I am always here for myself.

The Universe loves and cares for me.

Aloof and needy people are one common archetype.
The truth is that every relationship has been perfectly

designed to bring healing. When a relationship ends and you sit in your grief, you can either receive the healing and grow or remain stuck. The relationship is over, so of course you feel grief. But take a moment to think about the things you learned so that you can receive the gifts, or else you'll just do the same dance again with another person.

Uncovering the Gifts in a Relationship

Barbara was a healer when she met Craig, who worked in corporate sales. She was in her late 30s, and he was a couple of years older. He worked for a large company but also did astrology readings on the side. She loved that he was quirky and wanted a different life. He hoped someday to be a full-time astrologer since he hated his job of selling people things they didn't really want or need. He was only doing it because it had been his father's line of work.

Barbara, on the other hand, was an amazing free spirit. She had long blonde hair that seemed to draw the sunshine to her. Craig longed for her life because he felt that while hers was in color, his was a dull gray. He drove a company car, and she liked his stability—the fact that he got a paycheck every week.

But Craig was dissatisfied with his life and was determined to find a way out of his world and into hers. Barbara told him that the way to begin the journey was to find a spiritual master. That master for Craig turned out to be an American Indian who smoked clove cigarettes, so Craig began smoking, too. Barbara was shocked; she disapproved of smoking and couldn't believe he had taken it up. When she told him there would be no smoking in the house, Craig argued that he should be able to smoke in the den. So they compromised on that.

He also thought that he should stop accepting his regular paychecks. Saying "no" to the corporate world would surely help him advance in his creative one. Craig believed that the corporation was draining the life out of him, so he quit and gave up the company car and his salary. He wanted to earn a living as an astrologer, and although he got everything ready, the clients never came.

"How do you intend to build your business?" asked Barbara.

He had no definitive answer. He just thought that Spirit would bring him clients—that his practice would build on its own. He also thought that he didn't need material possessions. After all, if he had to go some-where, he could always use Barbara's car. She, however, hated the fact that now she would be responsible to pro-vide his transportation.

One day after he had been up all night reading the astrology ephemeris, Craig told her, "I won't be making money until late next year. That's what the signs say, so I guess I'll have to borrow money from you until then."

He didn't ask; he just informed Barbara, as if he had peered into the future. When her credit-card bill came, that was the last straw. Unbeknownst to her, she had been paying for Craig's cigarette habit all along. Barbara knew this no longer fit her picture. She went out and bought him a used car for $1,200 and said, "This is your gift. I encourage you to go live your dream."

He reluctantly left, and she felt betrayed and aban-doned, even though she had sent him away. She felt like Craig had done a bait and switch. As a healer, Barbara believed that in a relationship, two people were meant to grow together, and she could not understand how they had grown apart. His spiritual quest made her feel taken advantage of and used financially. In her grief, she was also very angry with herself for not putting her foot down sooner. She saw the signs that things were going in a bad direction but ignored them. She also gave Craig more latitude because she didn't want to interfere with the spiritual journey he was on.

After the breakup, she would tell herself, *What an idiot I was.* She bombarded herself with the question: *How stupid could I be?* She began to give a lot of energy to her own mistakes when one of her friends intervened and said, "You have to stop this, Barbara. You're not a foolish person, but you're portraying yourself as inept at life and relationships."

Barbara realized that her idea of people growing together was half right. Ultimately, people grow—maybe together, maybe not. But as a healer and spiritual person, she made the mistake of thinking that growth always meant growing toward each other rather than growing toward each other's *higher good.* She was finally able to see that her relationships were ruled by fear. Fear that she would be alone. Fear that her man would leave her. Once she was able to stop fighting the concept that something went wrong or that he was the wrong guy, she could see the lessons. She could begin to see that even what she perceived was wrong could still have healing lessons for her. She started to understand the difference between getting what you "want" and allowing things to unfold for a higher purpose. She now tries to live by the following affirmations:

Love guides all of my relationships.

My relationships move toward my highest good.

All is well in my relationships.

The person I am with has gifts to offer me.

Years later, Barbara and Craig reunited on Facebook. She had completed a psychology degree and was currently a psychologist with a private practice. Craig was preparing people to survive the end of the world, which he believed was to be in 2012. Looking back at the intersection of their lives, it was so clear to Barbara that it was not meant to last forever. The relationship had occurred so that she could see his world, he could view her world, and they both could move on to their personal destinies. Nobody failed. That's just the way that relationships are, even though we try so desperately to make them different or somehow deeper or more fulfilling.

After a breakup, sometimes we search for new love, so remember that a teacher will appear when you are ready for the lesson. When it's time for you to be in a relationship again, that "someone" will appear.

It's challenging for many people when they focus on others they're attracted to. They feel like they have romantic feelings for them, or they're just plain smitten. But the love and feelings in some cases are not returned. Remember, we always have a choice. We can continue to pursue those individuals, or we can release them to the Universe with love.

Fairy-Tale Thinking

In the movies, when the main character falls in love with someone but the affection isn't returned, he or she keeps pursuing that unrequited love. And in the end, the target of affection—usually at a big dressed-up public event—realizes that the main character is indeed the one! But in real life, most say, "No, thanks," or "Sorry, you're not my type."

What is your thinking in that situation? *She doesn't want me, but someday she will.* Or perhaps, *I will make him love me,* or *I will get him one day.* Can you just accept the truth? Why let your fairy-tale thinking manipulate the situation? This is a moment when you're struggling and should be grieving. Can you grieve the disappointment fully and be done? Why chase someone who doesn't want you? Why would you want to bring that kind of neediness into your consciousness?

Instead, consider the following affirmations:

A person who loves me back is on his way to me.

The right person for me will know who I am.

*I don't have to convince anyone to love me.
The right person will love me.*

The grief you feel at the end of a relationship is sometimes a misperception that things didn't work out and that your life is going wrong. Of course the loneliness hurts after a relationship ends, but allowing your thinking to focus only on the loneliness will make you even more miserable. Acknowledge it, and be open to more positive thoughts entering your consciousness.

Take a look at your grief, and ask yourself, *If every-thing is unfolding as it is supposed to, what else am I feeling?*

If you can separate yourself from the grief of the relationship, you can drop into a deep inner cavern of an old wound and then finally rid yourself of it. Under the grief, you may discover an abandonment issue that's repeating itself—perhaps a perceived rejection from a parent when you were young, or a first love that spurned you. The healing of these inner wounds won't necessarily guarantee that you'll get your next relationship right. But you may find the clarity to understand that relationships never really go wrong. If you find that ending a relationship is extremely hard, just know that you aren't alone. Most people know how to begin and end relationships, but rarely learn how to complete them.

Every relationship is assigned to you for your healing. Grief after any relationship gives you the window to heal your wounds and begin anew. Each relationship gives you an opportunity to face your fear and anger. But more important, they give you the chance to come closer to authentic healing and true love.

Ultimately, relationships, with their mysterious and wonderful forces, are our guides, teaching us all to love and honor one another—as well as ourselves. They may never produce the long-lasting emotional fix we may have hoped for, but in grief, after they end, they remind us that we are not broken or incomplete, and they can deliver us to healing. We let go of our earth-made agendas in loving relationships. We cast aside questions of who will love us and for how long. We transcend all breakups to find a love that is magical and divine, created by a force greater than us, just for us.

Many times a relationship doesn't fit your expectations. It's so easy to judge that the person or even the relationship is wrong. You say to yourself, *That was just a waste of time,* but there is no waste in the Universe.

If the Universe had sent you an amazingly sweet, loving person, and your consciousness was not ready for it, then that person would simply not have been right for you in that time. The individual in front of you right now—the relationship, the situation—was divinely designed for your healing. When you accept that he or she was the right person for this time in your life, you'll plant sacred seeds that will heal you in ways you cannot begin to imagine.

The Universe sends me the perfect
people for the perfect lessons.

Happiness is my destiny.

All people and all situations are
delivering me toward my higher good.

Tapping Into the Love Within

It's likely that you've often heard about self-love—that your greatest love is within you—so we would like to take some time and break down how and why self-love works.

You may wonder why we need to talk about loving ourselves in a chapter about grieving the loss of another person after a breakup. There is sadness and often loneliness that must be recognized and honored, but beyond that is an overwhelming emptiness that is more than the vacancy left by the other person. That pain often causes as much, if not more, suffering than the grief of the loss of the person. The overwhelming emptiness is not the other person being gone, but the lack of self-love.

Think of it like a huge tank: If yours is completely empty and someone comes along and fills it with affection and tenderness, you feel an amazing sense of love entering your life. Yet you also feel a desperate neediness, because your tank rises and falls dramatically with the ebb and flow of the relationship. Then, when the person leaves, you are left with nothing, and that kind of emptiness is gut-wrenching.

But what if you had your own reservoir of love? What if someone else coming into your life simply added to it? How different would your relationships be? Grief is a gauge that allows you to take note of how you're doing in this area.

Naomi met a really interesting guy named Gary at a singles' event. She loved that they met there because there was no guessing whether he was interested in meeting someone—that was the purpose of the event. They went out several times over the course of three weeks, and Naomi was enjoying getting to know Gary. She had no agenda that this would be forever; rather, she was just enjoying their time together.

At the movies, the couple ran into friends of Naomi's, who invited them to go dancing on Saturday night. They agreed to meet at a local club, and everyone had a great time. At one point, the other couple took out their camera phones to take some pictures. First they asked Naomi to take a picture of them. Then, Naomi took out her own phone and posed with Gary for a few photos.

Gary grabbed Naomi in his arms in a warm embrace while they were posing, and all of a sudden, she felt a huge rush of love. Her friend said, "One more picture just to be safe," and Naomi melted into Gary's arms.

The next morning, Naomi showed the pictures to friends who said, "Looks like you two were having fun." Naomi thought about the love she had felt when Gary put his arms around her. She thought about how different her perception was now, as opposed to what it would have been a decade earlier. Back then, she would have said, "I never felt love like I felt last night. Gary is amazing. He must be the one."

She had done so much inner work since then that she knew Gary didn't hold an incredible, unique love that was only accessible when she was with him. She knew that he had somehow triggered the love that was already within her. It was not *his* embrace that sent a rush of love from him to her. Rather, she made the unconscious decision to feel that depth of love. She also knew intellectually that while Gary was a great guy, after three weeks of dating, she knew she couldn't honestly say that he was the greatest love of her life.

At this point, you may be wondering if the relationship continued. Gary and Naomi did continue to date, and she would add that they dated sanely. She knew that she had avoided a huge trap that was a part of her old pattern. In the past, she would have believed that she had met the most amazing man, the one guy in the world who held the key to her deep love. She would have felt a neediness for the love that she believed only emanated from him . . . but now she knew better.

The point of this story may sound like a cliché, but no one out there is your source or holds the key to true love for you. True love is always inside of you, and you decide, consciously or unconsciously, whether you will allow yourself to access it. In grief, it's easy to believe that your love left with the person and you are now empty. But we're here to remind you in your loss that the love you accessed is still within you, ready and waiting. The next new person in your life won't find it for you, but you can experience it whenever you are truly open.

All the love I need is within me.

*Other people remind me of the deep
love I already have within.*

Healing the Past

Your mind is often at war with itself. It uses the people and situations around you to play out your inner struggles in the world in 3-D. Grief is a time when you can look back at the past and review the patterns in your thinking, but as we've already mentioned, to go back and simply relive it over and over is painful and nonproductive.

If you have the courage to look into your past without blame, criticism, and faultfinding, you can view how your thinking occurs and what it says. You can find clues as to the makeup of your behavior. That's how grief can provide you with a window of opportunity to not just look into how a relationship ended, but to also understand the thinking that built the relationship in the first place.

The next story is about Carla, who had the courage to look into her past as an observer. She realized that as long as she could remember, she was unhappy. "I'd like to say I was born that way—though highly unlikely—but for some reason, I was never a happy child," she said.

Carla always felt like a victim in her life and unknowingly kept up a pattern of unhealthy relationships followed by long bouts of grief. An example was when she was 28, and she and Ben (who didn't want to be referred to as her boyfriend) broke up.

Carla knew by society's standards that she was considered beautiful. Tall, athletic, fun, and smart, she also had varied cultural interests. Without her ego involved, she could see that she was "a catch," but that changed when she met Ben. She suddenly thought that she "was unattractive, undeserving of love, and unworthy." She came to believe that she would never be happy and find love. If she did, it would run a short course and end in grief.

She remembered, "I felt so broken. I ended things with Ben because he had already met someone else he was head over heels with—someone he was willing to actually call his 'girlfriend' and do things with that he never wanted to do with me." She felt that life was showing her that she was, in fact, not good enough. "The grief had me crying day after day, week after week," she said, "wondering where I'd gone wrong. I wondered why God and the Universe had to punish me over and over. Didn't I deserve love and happiness like others? Was I so different? My grief overwhelmed me, and I was almost fired from my job for my negative attitude."

And then it hit her. Carla was able to see externally how dateable she was—but, more important, she acknowledged that internally she felt empty, negative, and needy. She thought, *I wouldn't want to date me. I wouldn't want to be with someone who, despite having the potential for so much good, had such low self-esteem, disliked herself, and had no confidence. If I wouldn't date me, why would anyone else want to?*

She realized that it was high time for her to become who she wanted to be, or more accurately, who she really was. She found various versions of one affirmation and would recite them daily. She would say to herself:

I love myself.

I forgive myself.

I totally release all past experiences.

I am free.

Carla decided that she would "fake it" until she could "make it." She knew she would have to choose what a "loving person" would do. She understood that that was a better decision than embodying her negative past thoughts. It's similar to the saying from Alcoholics Anonymous: "You can act yourself into a new way of thinking more easily than you can think yourself into a new way of acting." It was a statement that made sense to her, since she knew she didn't fully believe in the wonderful person she was inside.

When Carla began to pay attention to her own negative thinking and replace it with something more positive, two moments stuck out in her mind. The first incident was when she was on a date, and she asked herself, *What would a confident me say in this situation?*

She was surprised that it came with such ease. Her date was staring into her eyes, and he blurted out, "You're so amazingly confident!"

She recalls, "It hit me in that moment that I was. There was some truth in faking it."

At 29 years old, Carla had reached a level of confidence that she hadn't ever known before. She wasn't aware of crossing the fine line between faking it and actually making it, but she knew something was changing. She had thought that the saying, "Fake it till you make it," was more about faking a feeling. She didn't realize that it was about doing something until her mind, body, and spirit were all in touch with a belief that was already in her. It may have been buried deep down and hidden away, but she realized that she was conditioning her body and mind to come back in tune with her self-truths.

The second moment happened right after New Year's Eve. Carla knew she had a lot of work to do on herself and thought that this year, her New Year's resolution would not be about places she wanted to go or things she wanted to do, but rather about whom she wanted to be. She told herself, *I want to be confident, loving, and happy.*

Carla saw herself as someone who walked down the street with a big smile on her face that radiated outward to others who would in turn smile a little more and get some extra bounce in their step.

All of her previous attempts at finding validation in outward sources (dating, jobs, and friends) had always backfired, and now she understood that she had to find these things in herself first. She felt driven to change her thinking, so she wrote the following on a piece of paper:

I love and accept myself.

I am worth it.

She taped that slip of paper on her bathroom mirror so it was the first thing she saw when she woke up. She repeated the affirmations when she brushed her teeth and applied her makeup. The phrases kept ringing through her head and her subconscious:

I love and accept myself. I am worth it.

Carla started doing this on January 1, 2012, but some time later, she realized she didn't need that piece of paper anymore. She didn't need to look at it because she was automatically repeating those words in her head every day, all day long. One year later, on New Year's Day 2013, she looked in the mirror, laughed, and said:

I love you.

I really, really love you.

"I really, truly felt it," she said. "For the first time in my life, I was able to look in the mirror and know that I genuinely loved myself. For someone who spent a lifetime in self-hatred, it was a magical feeling that I can't describe in words. I know I still have work to do and more love to give to myself and others, but the feeling of being able to love myself and attract better and more loving people into my life has been astounding for me.

My friends have noticed the change in the last year, and they say it's the happiest they've ever seen me."

Recently, Carla had a roommate, Ellen, move in who reminded her of herself a few years ago with her self-doubts and criticisms, always searching outward for her source of happiness and love. She suggested that Ellen listen to how terribly she was talking to herself, and told her how she herself had replaced her negative thoughts with positive affirmations that had really helped.

Her roommate's response was, "Yeah, yeah, that's a good idea," but Ellen never did anything about it. A few months later, after listening to her continue to berate herself relentlessly, Carla brought it up a final time, but she realized that her roommate just couldn't take that step. Ellen looked so lost. So Carla took a piece of paper and pen and wrote down some positive affirmations and gave them to her. When Ellen looked at what Carla had written down, she began to cry.

"Why are you crying?"

"Because they're not true," Ellen said. "I don't accept myself. I don't love myself."

Carla smiled and told her, "That's why they are called affirmations. Why don't you just fake it till you make it?" Carla had discovered that as much as she loved the feeling of giving her love to someone else, she loved the feeling of loving herself even more, and she tried to explain that to Ellen.

Ultimately, Carla knew her strength was in offering more positive options to Ellen and that her real power was to do it herself and model it for others. And she genuinely believed that *Now when a man comes along, he'll be a great addition to my life, but he won't define my life.*

Loving Yourself No Matter What

Shelly had been in a relationship with Bill for four years. She had felt that something was wrong for a long time but was too afraid to end things. She had told herself over and over again, "If I leave, I'll never find someone else." While she tried her best to gain Bill's love, she often felt depressed and discouraged because somewhere inside of her, she knew that trying to make Bill love her was impossible. She did everything she could think of, including buying him expensive presents, but she never felt like she was getting anything back. She really didn't think he loved her.

One night, exhausted from trying to be the perfect girlfriend, the perfect listener, the perfect everything to him, Shelly sat down on the floor in her bathroom and cried out of desperation. She thought, *I'm not good enough for him, I just don't deserve to be loved,* and *If I leave, I'll be alone forever.* Even as she sobbed on the bathroom floor, she knew somewhere inside that she wasn't being true to herself.

When Shelly stood up and looked at her face in the mirror, she saw deep grief and despair, and her heart went out to her own reflection. *I have to help that woman in the mirror,* she told herself. That was the first kind and loving thought she'd had about herself in years, and soon afterward she found the strength to break up with Bill.

At first Shelly was grief-stricken and even more desperate than before, so she reached out to a friend who gave her a book of affirmations. She cried while reading almost every page because the affirmations were the opposite of the mean-spirited things she had been telling herself. She realized that not only had her boyfriend been treating her terribly, but she was also treating *herself* the same way. Shelly went back to the same bathroom mirror, looked at her reflection, and said, "I love you."

It felt awkward at first, but it also felt right, so she continued. She soon realized that the more affirmations and mirror work she did, the more she was able to distance herself from her old way of thinking. She eventually saw the truth in that she did love herself, no matter what, which became the mantra she repeated for the first three months:

I love myself no matter what.

It was perfect for Shelly, because she knew that her mind could twist it around to say, "I would love myself if I weren't getting so old," or "I would love myself if I wasn't bad in relationships." Throwing in "no matter what" made all the difference for her as she discovered that she could be loved and love others all at the same time. She was surprised by how this inner work that seemed so small and unimportant could change her life. Shelly remembered all her judgments about looking old, but she didn't try to tell herself that she was young or looked youthful. That would be wrong because it would affirm that there was a better age for her to be than the age she was right now. Rather, she began to remove her attention from her inner critic and would affirm:

My spirit is youthful.

My outlook on life is always vibrant.

One day, people began telling Shelly how radiant she looked, and she also noticed that her life had become much better lately. She felt radiant! Sometimes, however, when the improvements scared her or her doubts would creep in, she would say:

I love myself no matter what.
Even if I'm scared, I love myself.

Even if I think my life is getting too good, I still love myself.

Battling her negative self-talk continues to be challenging for Shelly, but she learned how great it feels to wake up in the morning with a positive mind-set, seeing her body as something wonderful, and not whether or not it looks thin or fat. That was quite a revelation for her. Shelly found that even when she went out by herself, she didn't feel alone because the positive statements she repeated throughout the day were her constant companions. She put cards and reminders everywhere in her house and car that said:

My life is so good.

I am always grateful for my life, no matter what.

I love life, and life loves me.

In the end, she recognized that her breakup with Bill was a good thing because when she was alone, she found something way better than what another person could ever give her: *self-love.*

One of the quickest ways to nurture self-love and self-worth is through mirror work. Here's how you do it: Pick up a small mirror, and look at yourself. If you feel resistance, keep in mind that it's coming from the part of you that finds yourself unlovable. Gaze into the mirror anyway, and say to yourself:

I love you.

I will be good to you.

I love and accept you exactly as you are.

Give yourself the gift of practicing this every morning when you wake up and every evening before you go to bed. Make the agreement with yourself that whenever you pass a mirror throughout the day, you'll say something positive either out loud or silently.

You look good today.

I'm happy to be with you.

Good things are on their way to you.

Staying on Your Side of the Court

Picture your world as a tennis court, and you're playing with someone else. You only have control of your own thoughts, actions, and intentions—not what the other player does or thinks. So many times in grief, as well as in relationships, you may try to strategize, control, and operate from what the other person is doing. You have to bring your thoughts, words, and actions to your side of the tennis court. You have to focus on what you're doing and how the Universe is responding, and it all starts with your thinking.

Affirmations can help you maintain positive thoughts. After a breakup or when a relationship is winding down, pay attention to your thoughts. You might be thinking, *Maybe I could have kept the relationship casual,* or *He mistreated me, but everyone is human, and we all make mistakes.*

It may seem more loving or spiritual to think, *I should just accept him as he is, and be with what is,* but that thinking doesn't always serve you. Ask yourself, *When he was being his authentic self, did that bring love, light, and joy into my life? Or was it just a brief infatuation followed by a lot of misery?*

Sometimes your mind tells you to stay in a bad relationship because you think you need a placeholder—someone who you think loves you and is there for you. If you could see your thoughts as energy, what kind of energy are you attracting and perhaps settling for, and who is responsible for that energy? When a relationship ends, it's so easy to obsess about the other person: *Is she thinking about me? Does she miss me, too? Is she also analyzing the relationship like I am?*

All those thoughts are in the past—a past that probably didn't happen in the way you see it anyway. Think about bringing your thoughts and energy back to the present. Bring yourself back to your side of the tennis court because if your thoughts are all about someone else, who is managing *your* life? Who is taking care of *you?* What you probably wanted from your ex was to feel loved and cared for, but look at how you're *not* loving yourself. Look at how you're *not* taking care of yourself and how little you're giving to your own life. When you're obsessively thinking about someone, it's as if the person is taking up space in your consciousness without paying any rent.

As you reflect on the relationship with gentleness and compassion, notice how you settled for less, how you allowed yourself to engage with someone whose vibration didn't match yours. You may suddenly feel a pang and say, "Oh, but it did match." Even if that was true at one point, as you sit here heartbroken, it's not true anymore. As you move forward, bring your thinking to a higher place. Thank the Universe for this learning experience that resulted from the relationship, as it's helping you to heal and reminding you of who you truly are.

Begin to fill your mind with positive new thoughts. Instead of, *He just wasn't ready for a relationship,* try saying:

I am looking forward to having new relationships.

Instead of trying to figure out why he didn't want to be with you, think:

I attract people who want to be with me.

Remember that the Universe will test you. It may send you a few ambivalent individuals who don't know if they want to be with you, but be sure to stick with the affirmation:

I attract people who want to be with me.

When you're grieving, you can access a clearer vision of your self-esteem. Your self-talk becomes more apparent, and you can observe areas that need attention. This can be a powerful time of healing old patterns.

For example, let's say you go to a restaurant and order a tuna-fish sandwich, but the server brings you a bacon cheeseburger instead. If you have high self-esteem, you'll say, "This burger looks great, but I didn't order it. I ordered the tuna fish." You should get the sandwich you ordered because it brings you joy and makes you feel good about yourself. If you have low self-esteem, on the other hand, you'll probably be afraid to speak up and wind up eating the burger even though you didn't order it.

The same is true in relationships. Why would you accept a relationship that doesn't truly reflect who you are and what you want? If your significant other didn't bring you joy, then don't order that kind of relationship again. Try this exercise:

> Make a list of all the good things that you received from the relationship. For example, maybe you received love, companionship, and home-cooked meals. Make sure your list has at least five items.
>
> Now write down all the things that you wanted to receive but didn't get. For example, maybe you didn't get understanding, compliments, and encouragement. Make sure this list also has at least five items.

Once you've completed both lists, review the first one and give those things to yourself. Then take the second list, and send those items to your ex spiritually. If you wrote on your list that you didn't have a satisfying sex life, for instance, then wish your ex a fulfilling sex life in the future.

Or when your ex pops into your mind, send him love and wish him well. When your mind goes to his side of the tennis court, and you're thinking about his role in the relationship, remind yourself that you're on the wrong side of the court and say, "I lovingly heal my part in the relationship."

When you see that your ex is moving on with his life, remind yourself that you are the loving caretaker of *your* life, not his. Place your attention on where you can bring more to your relationship with yourself. Instead of energizing the misconnection with your ex, how about bringing more love and compassion to your relationships with your friends and family? Try this affirmation:

*Today I bring love to my life and
everyone I encounter.*

Use your review of the past to get to know yourself better right now and learn more about what you want. Sometimes reflecting on what did or didn't feel right is a good way to discover what you want and don't want in a relationship. Perhaps being with a partner who had little time for you didn't feel good. Maybe your being at home every weekend didn't feel good because you're more social than your partner wants to be. Or if you're passionate about current events, it probably didn't feel good to be with someone who wasn't all that concerned about what happens in the world.

Try pulling back to see the bigger picture and understand that all relationships are for healing. If you get no healing from the relationship, it will feel sad and pointless, and you'll be devastated by emptiness. But if you can see that this person came into your life to bring you to the next level, you will understand that you live in a Universe that is always conspiring for your good.

To receive the healing, repeat this affirmation:

My past relationship is complete, and I accept the healing.

These next affirmations will help you grow to the next level:

I attract relationships that are fulfilling and fun for me.

*If any relationships come my way that are not fulfilling,
I release them back into the Universe.*

When you grieve the loss of a relationship and look for ways to heal yourself, you will find that you can become the person you were truly meant to be. Grief triggers growth and can create a new foundation for you to receive even greater gifts from the Universe.

❧ ❧ ❧

One of the important lessons in a relationship is that you cannot give what you don't have. You can't receive love if you believe that you're unlovable. That's why growth is an inside job. The most magnificent love could come into your life, and if you judge yourself as unworthy, you won't be able to accept it. You may think that it's always about the other person, but ultimately, the capacity to give and receive love resides solely within you.

Hopefully, you've begun to look at your thought patterns in relationships. You can see how grief allows you to peer into your relationship dynamics. You can begin to not judge your past as wrong, but rather understand that the relationship has delivered you to this new starting point. In love, there is no wrong person. There are only perfect teachers. If your relationship is crashing, the only thing to do is to put on your oxygen mask and take care of yourself. Be gentle with yourself, and love yourself.

As we move on to the next chapter, we'll be looking at another form of relationship loss—marriage that ends in divorce—and continuing the healing journey.

∿

CHAPTER THREE

DOING DIVORCE
DIFFERENTLY

Many people feel that marriages have failed if they don't last forever. The same way in which some claim that the only truly complete life is one that lasts 95 years, lots of folks believe that the only successful and complete marriages are those that last "till death do us part." The reality is that marriages are successful and can heal regardless of how long they last, as long as they achieved what they were supposed to. When they're no longer needed, they are complete and successful. And yes, we realize that the idea of calling a marriage a success when it ends in divorce is a radical, unusual statement.

One of the truths of life is that happiness doesn't rely on relationships changing for the "better." When a marriage ends, two people have usually faced the reality that they can't change each other. They may have tried to change their spouse in order to make the marriage work, but after a divorce, the realization comes that this simply doesn't work.

When you see this, you'll stop asking, "What if she never changes?" and start believing, "What if she wasn't meant to change? What if we were supposed to get a divorce?" And if you want to be who you really are in life, shouldn't you allow your spouse to do the same, even if that means the marriage will end?

If you've been divorced you must ask yourself, *Was the love I gave and received based on how love was defined for me when I was a child? Did my parents fight all the time? Did they get divorced? Was this marriage truly the kind of love I wish to give and receive?* If you see love as being painful, complicated, a power struggle, or often cruel, then it's crucial that you examine why.

People often chose the one they want to marry because of choices they made growing up. This isn't to blame it all on your parents. It is commonly believed that by the time you turn 25 years old, you can no longer blame anything on those who raised you. But sometimes after a divorce, you go into a long period of analyzing why the marriage failed, what you did wrong, and so on. You may be surprised to look back and discover that what you watched growing up taught you, rightly or wrongly, how to manage relationships and marriage. The surprise is that you were already doing it 100 percent correctly because you did just what was modeled for you as a child. But you have the power to choose a new destiny for yourself and a new reality, postdivorce. Your thinking can lead you there in the same way that distorted thinking can keep you stuck.

Aidan, a 34-year-old attorney, was very successful in all aspects of his life except marriage. At a divorced men's group, he shared that he was exasperated with his love life and truly believed that he and his ex-wife belonged together. He went on to say that he had tried to develop a friendship with her since they had divorced two years prior, but whenever they were getting along—feeling friendliness or tenderness toward each other—he would end up saying something like, "See? I told you we should be together."

It was frustrating for him because he interpreted every good moment they had as a sign that reconciliation was their destiny. His ex-wife would say, "Why can't you accept that the marriage is over, and we're just friends?" He told the group that he knew if he found acceptance, which he did occasionally, everything would be all right.

"When you do get to the place where you find acceptance," the group leader asked him, "are you at peace?"

"I get to acceptance, but it doesn't last," Aidan answered. "It's not very peaceful, and it always seems to turn negative."

"It turns negative," the group leader pointed out, "because the moment you find acceptance, you also think, *Now will she come back?* That isn't true acceptance. That's just a manipulation your mind is doing when it tells itself, 'If I find acceptance, she'll come back to me.'"

Let's take a closer look at what Aidan is telling himself: "We *should* be together." In that comment alone, there are many negative messages, such as:

- The Universe has it wrong.
- Things are not okay as they are.

- My wife is not living the life she should.

- I am not living the life I should.

- Love has gone wrong.

- Things are not working out the way they're supposed to.

When we examine the situation, we see that Aidan has not allowed himself to mourn his loss, and he can't heal his grief as long as he believes that his divorce shouldn't exist. His denial does not serve him. In fact, it only prolongs the acceptance stage of the grieving process.

When you hear someone say, "It's easier to get over someone who died than someone who left me," this is one of those examples. When someone dies, there comes a point in your healing when you truly understand that he or she is not going to be with you again on this earthly plane. The person is gone. But when someone leaves you, the person is still out there but chooses not to be with you. Your distorted thinking could tell you, "It doesn't have to end. We could be together again." That distorted thinking in grief is often called *bargaining* and/ or *magical thinking*.

In the future, by the way, if both Aidan and his ex are still alive, they *could* end up together again. None of us knows what the future holds. But we do know that Aidan will never heal until he accepts the reality that he and his wife have divorced. Only then can he find healing in his grief.

Some affirmations he might consider saying to himself are:

The Universe gets everything right, including my divorce.

All things are unfolding as they are supposed to.

*My divorce does not constrict my
ability to love and be loved.*

My divorce has no power over my future.

*Some relationships will leave my life,
and some will remain.*

I am open to experiencing love in any form it exists.

Divorce can be an expression of healing. It may finalize a marriage ending, but it does not have to stagnate or block your ability to love. Aidan is using negative affirmations and negative thoughts to try to process what has happened. When he processes grief with negativity, he will come out with blame, guilt, and a belief that things have gone wrong. But he can shift his thinking—even if he needs to fake it for a while—to add those positive affirmations that will open his soul to the healing that needs to occur.

Sometimes you can't get to a place of positive thinking, and you may have to just work from where you are. So when Aidan says, "My wife doesn't understand that we should be together," he might consider not fighting the thought but shifting it to:

*My wife doesn't understand that we could be together.
And I will send her love and wish her well in her life.*

*I think we could still be married, but there
is a greater knowledge in the Universe.*

I don't know what could or couldn't happen.
I lovingly release my limiting beliefs.

The Universe is always moving me toward good.

Aidan had a clear picture of how his life was supposed to unfold, but he had to work through the reality of what he thought his life should look like versus
what it did look like. We all have these pictures. Some of
us call them expectations; some say that's just the way
things are supposed to be. No matter what we call it, we
must acknowledge that life deviates from those pictures
and expectations. It's like that saying, "We all have a
Plan A, but life is really about Plan B."

❧ ❧ ❧

Sometimes people come up against external blocks
to moving on with life after a divorce; these blocks are
often programmed by someone else, by society, or even
by religious beliefs.

Sharon, a nurse, worked in a Catholic hospital coor-
dinating services on their neurology unit. The hospital
offered Mass every day that was mostly for patients and
their families, but employees were also welcome to attend during their breaks. Sharon often chose to spend
her lunch hour in this way.

She and her husband, Paul, had been married for 22
years when he suddenly announced that he wanted a divorce. Sharon resisted, reminding her husband that they
were good Catholics and ought to find a way to work
out their differences instead. Yet despite her best efforts,
Paul ultimately continued with the divorce proceedings.

Sharon was so adamant that they *had* to stay together that she told the judge, "This is wrong! We're good Catholics, and we're supposed to work it out."

"Respectfully, your honor," Paul retorted, "when my wife first objected to the divorce, I agreed to go to counseling. We went for a few months, and I stand before you saying that I'm sorry, but it's just not working out. We have irreconcilable differences."

The judge granted the divorce. One year later, Sharon was still telling herself and others, "This never should have happened. God doesn't believe in divorce."

Besides the religious aspects of the situation, Sharon could find no healing as long as her mantra was, *This is wrong,* and *This never should have happened. God doesn't believe in divorce.* Some affirmations for her to consider are:

God knows what is best.

God can handle my divorce.

God can bless my marriage and my divorce.

God knows only love, so if you've been divorced, know that God does not recognize you as "divorced." God sees you as only love. Think of it in this way: Even if you believe that the Church and God have a problem with your marriage ending, you will most likely live many more decades. How do you want those years to look? Do you want decades of unhappiness? Decades of blame? Decades of guilt? It's your choice. You *can* have a sad chapter in your life called "divorce" but then move on to decades of compassion, happiness, and love.

That was Sharon's only reality-based choice: She could choose to live the rest of her life stuck in grief and regrets, or she could feel the loss fully and then open up to the idea of the rest of her life having a different story. It's important to choose thoughts wisely, and affirm only the positive ones.

Acknowledging Yourself

It was Jan's first Mother's Day without her husband, Gabe, and her grief was overwhelming. She was sad and depressed because he had left her for another woman—an older woman, in fact, which was a severe blow to her ego. She'd thought she was the perfect wife, so she couldn't understand how Gabe could do this to her and their four-year-old son, Corey. "I felt so abandoned, lonely, and worthless," she recalled.

As Jan washed the dishes, she remembered how her husband used to treat her like a queen on the holidays. He would cook a special Mother's Day breakfast and then celebrate with gifts and special outings. But this year, she was at home alone with Corey, washing dishes. In her grief, she fell to the floor devastated and started to cry, planning how she would end her life and end the pain she was feeling. At that moment, Corey walked into the kitchen and gently touched her shoulders with his small hands.

"What's the matter?" he asked.

"I can't do this anymore, Corey," she said, quickly trying to dry her tears.

"It's gonna be okay, Mommy," he said sweetly. Jan looked over at him and sighed, remembering that she had just considered leaving him by ending her life.

Corey helped her get up off the floor, and she thanked him and gave him a big hug. He smiled and went back to his room where he'd been playing with his toys.

Jan looked up toward the ceiling and said, "Why me, Creator? I need your help to find out why I feel the way I do." She prayed that night for guidance and drifted into a deep sleep.

The next day she went to work, where she was responsible for reviewing the professional/personal development requests from the staff of her company. After a short time, she noticed a flyer on her desk. One of the employees was asking to attend a self-help healing workshop. Jan picked it up and told herself, *I really do need healing.* But she realized that she needed to heal not only her grief over her husband, but her entire life as well. She read the flyer and called the employee who wanted to go to the workshop and asked if she could join her.

"When I first walked in," Jan said, "I wasn't sure what to expect. There were about nine or ten of us at someone's home, and I thought I would just observe and take notes. But by the time the workshop ended on Sunday afternoon, I felt a whole lot better than when I was sitting on my kitchen floor. I was learning to grieve the loss of my husband and heal myself by sending him love. Even more important, I was sending *myself* lots of love."

She practiced the following affirmations:

I will feel the sadness in my grief.

When I bring myself to my grief, it is healing.

In my sadness, I love myself.

After a few weeks of repeating the affirmations, Jan began to experience small moments of real happiness. Her grief didn't disappear, but it took on a softness she hadn't felt before. She never knew that she had to learn to love herself. She had never been taught how to do so because she'd been brought up not to express her feelings or set personal boundaries.

"Starting on that day," Jan remarked, "I continued my journey toward self-discovery and embraced it with open arms!" That weekend workshop had given her a jump-start to affirm that everything was happening for her highest good, and she believed that out of that situation, only good would come.

When she got home, she posted affirmations all over the house. The first one had come from her son:

It's gonna be okay, Mommy!

She also wrote:

I will feel my grief but not wallow in it.

Everything is happening for my highest good.

Out of this situation, only good will come.

Whenever Jan's thinking started going downhill, she walked over and looked at an affirmation as if she were seeing it for the first time. "I would stare at it," she said, "and try to really take it in. Then I sat down and repeated it over and over."

On her bedroom mirror, she posted:

I am safe.

In the bathroom was:

I love and forgive you.

The simple process of accessing her inner wisdom was what helped her feel empowered in her grief instead of being victimized by it. She even asked Corey to post his own affirmations, and together they would decorate and color them. He drew a lot of pictures of the sun shining, and Jan created this affirmation:

The sun is always shining.
It is always illuminating the good.

A year later, Jan remembered her last Mother's Day and thought how foolish it was to believe that the joy of the holiday came solely from her ex-husband. "It's all about my wonderful boy," she said, "who told me, 'It's gonna be okay, Mommy.' I'm teaching him that this is our special day, and what an honor it is to be his mother. Then we go out and celebrate. I could have never pictured this a year ago."

For Jan, because her son was so young, Mother's Day had been about her husband celebrating her motherhood. In time, there would have been a natural transition from her husband planning the day's events, to her son and her husband doing it together. Eventually, as Corey grew older, he would have taken it over and done it himself. The divorce sped up this process and caused Jan to find her own inner celebration of her

YOU CAN HEAL YOUR HEART

motherhood. In a way, it became more pure, and this was a true life lesson because she realized that being a mother was an aspect of herself that she always had the power to acknowledge on her own, regardless of whether her husband was there or her child participated in the celebration. When Jan reflected on her grief, she realized that no matter how sad she felt, she would always have herself.

When Grief Becomes Complicated

Despite our best efforts regarding grieving and healing, Life will sometimes throw us a curveball.

Bob and Marilyn, both in their 40s, had been married for 20 years. Bob was an outgoing kind of guy, always attending events and doing everything he could. Marilyn, on the other hand, was happy just being at home. Socializing with Bob was not her cup of tea, and in time, they began leading separate lives, seeing each other solely at bedtime and offering a short rundown of their days. Soon, leading their separate lives caused them to take on a sense of being roommates rather than being husband and wife.

Marilyn began to think she wanted more, realizing that she did want to do things and go to places but not the same things or places that interested Bob. Marilyn still loved her husband, but she saw that the marriage didn't fit any longer, and she wanted a life apart from him. What she'd feared the most was becoming a reality when she realized that she wanted a divorce. Thus began a yearlong process of talking. While Bob felt that they could work it out, Marilyn was willing to try but wasn't convinced that it would help. She eventually filed the divorce papers.

After the divorce was finalized, they remained friends, but in his grief, Bob was falling into "magical thinking" as he hung on to the idea that someday they would get back together.

Then the unthinkable happened about a year after they separated. Bob suffered a massive heart attack at work. The paramedics rushed him to the hospital and saved his life. But when he woke up, although he looked fine, he had sustained brain damage that resulted in short-term memory loss. He remembered the past and the big picture, but he had completely lost the last few years.

Bob's friends hoped that in time, his memory would come back, and for the first few months, Marilyn was by his side, happy to help. It brings to mind the popular movie *50 First Dates,* starring Drew Barrymore and Adam Sandler. In the film, Drew Barrymore's character has short-term memory loss, so each time she goes out with her love interest, played by Adam Sandler, it's as if they're on their first date. In Bob and Marilyn's case, because of the brain damage, he had forgotten all about the divorce and thought he was still married to Marilyn. As he grew stronger and she was there less and less, he would ask her where she'd been, and she had the grueling task of having to tell him again and again that they were divorced.

If I were a really good person, Marilyn thought to herself, *I would just move back in with him as if we were still married and take care of him.* Some days, she thought she should lie to him and let him believe that they were together, but she didn't want to pretend. She had dreamed of finding happiness after her divorce, but now she didn't think that was possible. She felt she was in a no-win situation and, as a result, her negative thinking was creating even more unhappiness.

What do you think about this? Do you think she should have lied to Bob and moved back in with him? When this kind of situation occurs, it's important to change your mind-set from "I can't find happiness" to:

I can find happiness in any situation.

I will find happiness whether we are married or not.

If Marilyn could bring a loving, whole, complete self to the situation, the framework of it would have the possibility of bringing happiness to all. She tried it, and when she let go of the "shoulds" and began to find her happiness, she would visit Bob in a good mood, and he soon stopped asking about their marriage. Perhaps because she no longer held anxiety about Bob's questions, he no longer needed answers.

Today, Bob still doesn't remember much about the last few years, but he has discovered a new normal. When Marilyn finally found peace in the divorce after everything happened, Bob seemed to have found peace, too. Now she talks about how happy she is to visit and how glad she is that they're still in each other's lives after all these years.

Grieving Through a Betrayal

We can't really talk about relationships ending or divorces happening without a discussion on betrayal.

While betrayal in and of itself can be hard to understand, even harder to comprehend may be the fact that being betrayed can sometimes offer us the greatest growth.

The idea that someone you gave your heart and soul to—the person who knew the real you and vice versa, or so you believed—would betray you is a horrific thought. The person who is most important to you, the one with whom you shared your most intimate self, has now shared him- or herself with someone else. It could have been for an hour or a night, or perhaps months or even years while you were together.

One of the first elements people often deal with in this kind of grief is how they found out. Did your loved one make a confession, or did it come out accidentally? Did you seek out the truth? Trying to get details about it often makes the wound worse because you'll use the information to further hurt yourself. Your partner may have betrayed you once, but with the details, you can play their transgression over and over in your mind. A tough question to ask yourself is if you were always suspicious in nature, or whether the news was a total surprise. It's interesting to go back and find the space you were in before you found out, which can sometimes help you uncover your part in what happened.

In terms of the actual healing of your grief, how you found out is somewhat inconsequential, but in terms of your thinking, it can be significant. Don't expect to see your role in the betrayal when you are in the acute part of the grief. Sometimes, months or years later, people are able to look back and say, "I was very suspicious. I think I was hoping it would end and knew on some level that our relationship wasn't meant to be." However, many struggle with this concept because when the words *your role* are used, they think the message is that the one who was betrayed was to blame. What we're really saying is that while no one wants to go through a betrayal, the experience is something that your soul can use for its evolution and healing.

There is another element to discuss here, not for the purpose of wallowing in grief, but to get it out and release it for healing. One of the first things that the betrayed person asks is, "Do you still love me?" In some ways, this is an inquiry, but in other ways, it's a deep evaluation of self. *Am I worth loving? Do I mean something to you? Did you ever really care?* It's hard to stomach the fact that your loved one's actions don't necessarily determine whether he or she loves you or not.

It's common spiritual wisdom that if there was a moment of real love in the relationship, then that was the ultimate truth—there *was* love. If you know love existed at one time, then the love was real, and the betrayal and everything that went with it will eventually, hopefully, disappear into the background. Years later, when exes see each other again, they often realize that the love is what lasts, and everything else fades. It may just become a fondness you feel for that person because you were a part of his or her history.

Remember, though, that you may not have this realization yet (or anytime soon) because you're upset. If you haven't, we hope you will take this as an invitation to release some of that anger. After all, your anger doesn't really hurt your partner—it is only toxic to you.

❦ ❦ ❦

Daisy had been with Cliff for five years. Their marriage had had its ups and downs but mostly ups. Daisy had imagined that someday, if their sex life waned, it would be her doing. She knew she might not always be as sexual as she was years ago, and she pictured the stereotypical married-couple dialogue when one day she might utter the words, "Not tonight, honey. I have a headache."

It caught her by surprise, however, when Cliff started saying, "Not tonight, honey. I'm too exhausted." Of course it was no big deal at first, but then his excuses seemed to grow: his back was hurting him, he was stressed out about work, and so on.

After Daisy determined a clear pattern, she immediately put the blame on herself. She thought, *If Cliff doesn't want to be intimate with me, it must be because I'm not as attractive as I used to be.*

So Daisy went into a period of getting herself in shape, as she imagined that maybe she had gotten too relaxed at home, going without makeup and wearing comfy pajamas instead of lingerie. She didn't know how things should be in a marriage, but she knew she didn't want to be the typical dowdy wife.

Yet months after her external makeover, Cliff was even less interested in sex than he'd been before. When she brought it up, he would say, "Don't be silly, honey. It's natural, it happens. I still love you. Everything is fine."

"It's not about how you look," one of Daisy's friends told her. "When we're first in a relationship, we find the guy so interesting. Every story he tells is new and fascinating. But after a few years, his stories become old and repetitive. Daisy, you have to treat Cliff like you just met him."

Thus began Daisy's rediscovery of Cliff. She hung on his every word, acting as if his old stories were new and exciting . . . but still nothing changed. Finally, when it had been 11 months since they'd had sex, an exasperated Daisy said, "Cliff, I've done everything I can to be attractive to you. Do you see that? I've gone to the gym, I wear makeup all the time, I wear lingerie around you. I've done everything I can to make you feel like a man and show you that you're the most interesting thing to me. For God's sake, what is it? It can't be headaches, or that you're always tired and work is stressful. Are you sleeping with someone else?" She threw it out there, never expecting it to land.

Her husband looked down at his feet.

Stunned, Daisy said, "Why are you looking down? Oh God, don't tell me you're sleeping with someone. Are you?"

"I'm sorry," he said.

Daisy couldn't believe what she was hearing. "Who is it?"

"My secretary."

"Your secretary? Could it be more stereotypical?!"

After a series of arguments, separation, and then ultimately divorce, Daisy found herself in a world of betrayal and grief. After a few months, her denial had subsided, and she was feeling the full fury of her anger. At any given moment she would think, *How dare he let me go to the gym and try to have a better body for him while he was admiring someone else's? That jerk had me rushing to the bathroom the moment I woke up to put on makeup. He let me think that I wasn't enough, or that it was his stress from work.*

Her internal dialogue changed from day to day, but it went along these same lines: *And I found his dumb stories interesting. If I heard them once, I heard them a thousand times.* And then her grief took the form of self-blame. *How stupid was I to think that if I looked better, he would turn into a nice guy? How stupid was I for loving him? How stupid was I for caring?*

It is important to realize that what has happened *has* happened. In grief, we understand that we can't change the past, but we can change the way we think about it. In terms of the past, Daisy could change her thinking. She did not have to focus on the betrayal. We know this is hard to do, but it's well worth it. It's not that you would be denying the betrayal; rather, you would be focusing on your strengths. Instead of just thinking, *Cliff betrayed me,* Daisy might affirm:

Despite Cliff's actions, I still loved fully.

Or when she beat herself up mentally, instead of thinking how stupid she was, she could think:

My instincts were good.

Instead of thinking the entire relationship was a betrayal, she could say:

The love was real.
The relationship just wasn't meant to last.

In time, she'd be ready for more advanced thinking:

Ultimately, no one can betray me.

Who I am is beyond betrayal.

As Daisy continued her affirmations, she began feeling a lot of resistance to them. She needed to remember that they were where she wanted to be, not necessarily where she was. The resistance meant that she just had more anger to release. So besides reciting the affirmations, she needed to honor her anger and allow it to move through her so that she could release it.

She found peace knowing that she did everything possible in terms of looking her best and going to the gym. In the bargaining stage of grief, some women are haunted by questions like, "If I hadn't let myself go, would he have been faithful?" or "If I had worn makeup and put on sexier clothing, would he still have had an affair?" But they eventually reach the depression stage of their grief, realizing that *yes,* their spouses still would have cheated. It wasn't about them.

The only real betrayal is when we forget our true selves and our authentic self-worth. In the end, others may do well or make mistakes, but we can retain our self-worth and remember that in relationships, sometimes we lower our standards and stoop to behavior beneath us. And maybe we do things to get back at our spouses. Therefore, we may have to forgive and release ourselves from the binds of those who have hurt us.

When you forgive your ex for cheating on you 15 years ago, you're not saying that it's okay to hurt people. You are saying, however, that you understand that the other person made a mistake—that everyone makes mistakes—and you're no longer going to define yourself or your entire marriage by that mistake.

Moving from Grief to Grace

Molly thought about the possibility of a new reality, postdivorce. She knew she wanted more than to come away angry and bitter, so she found a positive way to overcome the negative circumstances that happened in her life. She came to believe that she created an experience of betrayal in her life in order to come into wholeness. Admittedly, it took time—much processing and a lot of self-forgiveness—for her to truly believe that statement. Let's look at how she got there.

Her husband, Mike, cheated on her and ended up living with the woman right after he and Molly split up. Because the pain of loss was so crippling, she was willing to try anything to feel better. A friend suggested that she try to love the grief and realize that it was there to heal the pain. She also reminded Molly to be gentle with herself.

Molly remembers how she felt back then. "I started out by lying on the couch all day, treating myself to a movie. I made my daughter a quesadilla many days in a row because I couldn't muster the energy for anything more. I spent every morning in the shower crying, releasing the pain. Then I began telling myself what a great job I was doing. I cut myself a massive amount of slack because I decided that I was worth my own love.

"Now I see how my life had been conspiring for me to realize all of this. It was never about getting the love from the outside—it was an inside job all along. I had been to the self-help classes, read all the books, and heard all the right ways to 'do' life. But this wasn't an experience of my mind; it was a journey of my heart."

Molly had never experienced any real self-compassion before the betrayal. She was her own harshest critic, the most oppressive version of herself, so there were no surprises when it happened outwardly. Her skin would already be so thick that any kind of disappointment would pale in comparison to the self-constructed wall against love and life she had created in an effort to protect herself from the hurts manufactured out of the harsh landscape of life. But the pain knocked her over.

"Love was the glue of the Universe, which I had not experienced firsthand," she said. "It had been there all along, but I had not let myself awaken to it. And when I judged my circumstances harshly by saying, 'See, you're just a scorned woman, a horrible mother, left by your husband. You drove him away! You deserve a crappy life,' I produced a sense of being against myself. I needed betrayal to move me beyond the idea that life was what it seemed.

"I allowed myself to be in that place, trusting that the good would come out, looking deeper and allowing myself to surface from the storm and claim my life and the blessings of this situation."

Not long ago, Molly was in her therapist's office, when for the first time, she came face-to-face with the woman her former husband had cheated on her with. She said, "Basically, all I could do was weep tears of gratitude for her. If she had not come forward so my own drama could unfold, I might not have the compassion for myself, my world, others, and the collective journey we took. That woman helped me to trust my life. The heartbreak, betrayal, loss, sorrow, grief . . . it all enabled me to trust my life."

How could what she once labeled as so bad be so life-giving? Molly is waking up to all of the fullness of life as she affirms, "When I let go of attachments to how things should unfold and just let myself be, I was no longer a victim to life's circumstances. My mind may have told me otherwise, but my heart led the way. This other woman was an integral character in my own life's journey."

It seemed to Molly that she was undeserving of the riches of love. But eventually she was able to include herself and everyone else in her definition of what was divine, tender, loving, patient, and forgiving—all of them new attributes for her. In this, she finally accepted full responsibility for the troubles in her life, and she realized that this was the key.

"Never can I blame anyone or anything for my life circumstances," she said. "I wavered for months and months with this foreign concept." It was so radical to her and somewhat overwhelming to know that she might accept her life as her own and not blame others for her pain and suffering. But she wanted peace, and that meant letting go of being against herself and others. That meant letting go of what was right and wrong (the other woman was "wrong" because she hurt Molly), and she really started believing the Universe was conspiring toward her wholeness. She saw that she could muster bits of compassion for herself and was finally able to let go of the belief that she had done something wrong.

Molly couldn't be against herself and believe that the world was against her, so she decided that everyone she met—close friends, casual acquaintances, and even "the other woman"—was an integral part of the movie of her life that was propelling her toward wholeness. And for that, she became very grateful.

"When I met 'the other woman,'" Molly said, "I told her how much I had hurt. I was honest with my story. I apologized for ever wanting to hurt her or wanting others to hate her. I thanked her. I did this for myself. I, too, make mistakes, and this person was no less than me. It was only because I was hurting and suffering so much that I wanted the world to hate her and what she had done. Before, I thought my suffering might ease if she suffered, but, in truth, I freed myself by forgiving her. I waited until I was truly ready, and I was scared to death.

"It wasn't easy to face this woman, to be honest and cry for an hour straight. But I wanted to live to the fullest of my potential, and I wanted life to meet me where I met it. And so life will keep handing me my lessons toward grace. It all is for grace because I chose it."

Many affirmations that Molly uses are:

May this work out for the highest good of all concerned.

I deserve a beautiful life.

My lessons in life lead me toward grace.

I attract a good life that creates wonderful experiences.

As Molly has demonstrated, when we heal our thoughts, everyone in the situation rises to a higher level.

Putting Children First

So much of your thinking is shaped by your past, especially your childhood. Do you effectively spend so much time trying to heal the negative thoughts of your childhood that you don't think about your children when you divorce? They are in grief also, as they're losing that picture they've held of a mom and dad always together.

It's vital that you bring loving thoughts to your children's world during this time. If not, your self-examination becomes self-indulgence. In love, it's natural to let your walls down, but in divorce, the walls are often reconstructed even stronger.

What are walls, actually? They are the separation from another human being. When children are involved, you need to remember that even though you built the wall in response to your pain over your ex, your children are left grieving, trying to navigate these walls that they don't understand. If you allow these thoughts to rule your world, separation becomes the law of the land. In order to heal this, you must bring your thoughts back to love for your children and yourself. However, it's not an easy task when you believe that building walls protects you.

Take the example of Jackie, whose marriage had ended bitterly. There was so much deep-seated hurt, anger, and resentment on both sides that she and her ex-husband, Matt, were barely speaking.

This past December marked the first Christmas in which they had to figure out how to spend the day separately. Jackie was torn between her anger and resentment toward Matt and her deep desire to be with their daughter, Amanda, who was not yet two years old. Jackie realized that this was a special time in her daughter's life, and the thought of not being with her on such a momentous day ripped at her soul. She felt torn and conflicted like never before, and her heart ached at the thought of them not being together.

So she and Matt came up with a plan: Jackie would have Amanda in the morning, and Matt would take her in the afternoon, although they'd have to do an uncomfortable handoff at noon. Jackie was upset by the thought of this and spent the day thinking up various ways to distract herself from her sorrow at not being able to be with her baby the entire time. In her grief, she had honored and felt her loss, but she also needed to affirm some different possibilities for the day and her future.

She said, "I prayed and prayed, and knew I needed a powerful affirmation. I didn't want this anger and sorrow. Then one statement struck my heart at its core:

I forgive you, and I set you free.

"I think I said that affirmation a thousand times a day. I said it when I thought about my ex-husband, and I said it to myself. I knew I was judging myself for my anger and resentment, and I was even judging myself for judging others."

Keep in mind how upset Jackie had been feeling. It's very hard to pray and hold on to hate at the same time, however, and it was practically impossible for her to recite an affirmation a thousand times a day and still be distraught. For Jackie, the affirmation was working.

"A couple days later," she said, "my mind was in a new place, and I found myself inspired by love. I knew what I wanted to do. I invited Matt to spend Christmas morning with my family before he took Amanda to his place and they had their time together. I let him know that he was free to say no, but that he was also very welcome to join all of us. I made it clear that we'd all love it if he were there. And then I let it go."

Her ex-husband said yes immediately, and they had a wonderful day. Jackie realized that there was nothing her daughter loved more than being with all of her family, and there was nothing Jackie loved more than seeing so much joy in her daughter's sweet little face.

Jackie also got some surprises that morning. "It was a miracle," she said. "Watching them together, I found myself appreciating my ex-husband and the role he plays in my life, and the fact that he's always been a great father to our daughter. It was a wonderful day, but it wasn't over yet. When it came time for Matt and Amanda to leave, I noticed that my heart wasn't heavy—it was light and free. There were no hooks or chains, no sadness, only an ever-present feeling of love and gratitude. I walked them to the car, and after I said good-bye to my daughter, I hugged my ex and thanked him for coming. I wished him a Merry Christmas and told him to enjoy his time with his daughter. And I meant every word."

Jackie found that something as simple as an affirmation brought an incredible amount of love and joy into many people's lives that day. It would not have been the same for everyone if Amanda had not been there, and Jackie realized that it wasn't just about her.

Healing the Grief of Divorce

When divorce happens, it's very common to search for the reasons that caused it. Who did what to whom? But remember that these reasons are part of the smaller story. There's a much bigger story going on about your love, your life, and your soul's journey. Your goal is not to rid yourself of grief, but instead to see happiness in your future and to remove all the barriers—the things that don't serve you—between you and that happiness.

You have to search for a way to forgive your spouse. As hard as that may be, it will ultimately set you free. Holding a grudge is like a poison *you* drink, hoping that the *other* person will die. If there's a third person involved in the divorce, do your best to forgive him or her, too. Forgiving everyone involved may be an unbelievable challenge, but your willingness is all it takes to begin.

I am willing to forgive.

In healing the grief of divorce, you must take responsibility for your life. For you to fully heal and allow the grief to heal you, you cannot remain a victim. In your marriage and in your relationships, when anything happened that you perceived as wrong or bad, there was always one common denominator—*you*. You were present in every situation, so you must take some amount of accountability. Even if you can't find your part in a particular situation, perhaps in the bigger picture you can find some truth in the thought that your soul has chosen many different types of experiences for you to learn and grow.

Ultimately, you must give yourself the love you seek. That doesn't mean we're asking you to fill yourself up with self-love so that you never need or want another relationship. We hope that if you can find love inside of you, you won't show up for the next chapter of your life as an empty tank needing to be filled. Rather, you will be a whole person full of love, and you can bring that love to every situation and every person you encounter.

Grief is a time of mourning all that has been lost— the dreams that have been shattered, and the loss of hope for the marriage you thought you were going to always have. However, when you can arrive at sweet acceptance that what has happened did actually happen, you will find that grief is also a time of renewal, rebuilding, and reforming. You now have the opportunity to create yourself anew. Who will you be after the divorce? Don't just leave a void for others and your past to fill and define you. Choose who you want to be. This is a new chapter, and you have the opportunity to start again. If you're thinking, *It's too late for me to start again,* just know that that is only a thought—and one that isn't true. If you're still residing on the planet, it's never too late for you to start over. Here's a great exercise to help you get started:

> Think about all the negative words that describe how you're feeling after a divorce, such as *sad, hopeless, pathetic, unloved, unwanted,* and so on. Write them down on a piece of paper, and put it in an envelope. Then find a ritual that will truly help you release those words for good. Be sure to do whatever feels right to you in the moment. You might pray over the envelope, or you could choose to burn it. Ultimately, it's about releasing those words and knowing that they don't express the truth about who you are.
>
> Next, think about all the positive words that describe how you could feel and who you could be, and write them down. Remember,

they don't have to be true yet. They only have to feel right and express who you would like to become. Here are some examples:

Amazing
Courageous
Inspired
Lovable
Worthy
Passionate
Openhearted
Fun-loving
Sweet
Adventurous

Of course, there are many, many others that you can use—stick to what feels right for you. When you're finished, write an "I am" sentence for each of your words so that you really immerse yourself in them. For example:

I am amazing.
I am courageous.
I am inspired.
I am lovable.
I am worthy.
I am passionate.
I am openhearted.
I am fun-loving.
I am sweet.
I am adventurous.

Make copies of these sentences, and post them all over. Absorb them, live them! And remember this affirmation to help keep you on your path when you think of your life postdivorce:

*I am focused on the positive
possibilities of my future life.*

You can treat divorce like any other stage of life. You can label it as good or bad, and it can be viewed as a period of tragedy or growth. All marriages can be successful, regardless of how long they lasted. No ex-spouse holds control over your future. Only you do.

Your good will come from seeing the potential for happiness in your future. You can achieve this by releasing the past with your spouse; practicing forgiveness; putting your children first; and, perhaps for the first time, putting *yourself* first. If your beliefs surrounding your divorce are clouded by certain religious beliefs, this may be a great opportunity to find the good in your religion. Many people were brought up with wonderful theology, and others were brought up with toxic beliefs. Divorce can be a time to be still and really tune in to the values of God, not dogma.

Divorce is an ending, but it can also be the start of something new. And remember, what you give your attention to will grow. Do you want to live in the past, or do you want to focus on the present and your unlimited potential for love and happiness?

∼

CHAPTER FOUR

THE DEATH OF A
LOVED ONE

Everyone experiences loss, but the death of a loved one is unmatched in its emptiness and profound sadness.

We continue to examine the meaning of death because death is critical to the meaning of life. Some believe that death is an enemy that eventually triumphs over us—a horrible trick of nature that brutally defeats us. If you buy into these beliefs, then your life is meaningless. However, if you understand that you are born, you flourish, and when your time comes, you die, you will live from a meaningful place and also die in a meaningful way.

You must keep in mind that although your loved one has passed on, your life continues. A new, unexpected world appears before you, one in which they will no longer be physically present. On some level, you may feel they continue to live on spiritually. They do! Just as you cherished them when they were present, now you must love them in their absence.

Your loss and the grief that accompanies it are very personal, different from anyone else's. Others may share the experience of their losses in an attempt to console you in the only way they know how. For you, however, your loss reflects a unique love that you experienced. Your grief is a reflection of that love—evidence of that love. Every tear is validation that you have loved and cared deeply. No one should or want to take that away from you.

Yet neuroses and fears can get mixed up in those feelings of grief. Without realizing it, you may turn on yourself, which is why you must learn to pay attention to your thinking. Your thoughts can comfort you, but at times, they can also imprison you in your pain and create unnecessary suffering. The only way out of the pain is through it. You must feel it, but not stay in it or live your life from it. The only way to feel love when you're grieving is to stay aware of how you treat yourself during the loss.

Time to Release the Guilt

Ryan and his wife, Kim, met each other in law school. She was helping to pay for college by working in the library where he often went to study. Ryan's library visits moved from afternoon hours to evening hours, coincidentally matching Kim's work schedule. Eventually, she thought, *This guy is either a really great student who studies a lot, or he likes me.*

Each night, she would walk by Ryan at 9:45 and say, "Fifteen minutes till closing. Time to go."

And on one evening, he replied, "It's time for us to go for coffee."

Their coffee date turned into dinner dates, and before long, they were an item. After graduation, they got married. Kim's mother had been a teacher, so it wasn't a surprise when Kim was drawn to educational law. Her cases were mostly those of child advocacy, although once in a while, she handled wrongful-termination lawsuits for teachers. Ryan, on the other hand, went into real-estate law.

They raised three kids together, and when they were both in their 50s, they took a ten-day cruise to the Panama Canal. One afternoon after sunning herself on the ship's deck, Kim was in the shower when she happened to find a lump in one of her breasts. Certain that it wasn't there before, she was slightly worried and very annoyed that such a thing would show up when she was trying to enjoy her vacation. She decided to keep it to herself because it was likely nothing, and she didn't want to unnecessarily upset her husband. She also knew that she could manage her own concerns and put them aside for now, but Ryan would immediately become a basket case.

When they got home, Kim made an appointment with her gynecologist but still didn't mention it to Ryan. She decided that she'd tell her husband after she had gotten a clean bill of health. Unfortunately, she didn't get the news she was hoping for. She was soon diagnosed with stage IV breast cancer, and she and Ryan were both in shock. Kim had been in the habit of checking herself regularly, and she never found anything unusual before. How they had missed the first three stages and gone directly to stage IV was beyond their comprehension.

They immediately placed their focus on the most aggressive chemotherapy regimen there was, as well as complementary therapies. Although Kim's body was handling the treatments well, there were times when she'd say to Ryan, "I think dying would be easier than this." After multiple rounds of chemotherapy, it was time to check her follow-up test results. She underwent multiple lab tests and a PET scan (an imaging technique that can show whether cancer is advancing or retreating). Sadly, the results showed that her cancer was very aggressive, and the chemo had done little good.

One of her doctors suggested that they might consider hospice care, but Ryan and Kim thought that was a big jump. They believed there was more to be done and wanted to try everything. They consulted a number of other doctors, but the answer was always the same. Finally, Kim and Ryan had to acknowledge that her body was clearly winding down, and they signed on for home hospice. Kim was afraid that she wouldn't like having nurses around and that she'd feel invaded, but the nurses were lovely.

One day she told her husband, "Promise me that when my time comes, you'll let me go."

"Only if I can see you again somewhere, somehow," Ryan replied. "But I don't want to find that you've been dating someone else in the afterlife."

After a few weeks of pain control and symptom management, Kim had more energy and was feeling better than she had in months. She and Ryan would joke,

"Who knew that hospice care would be the thing that made me feel better!"

For the next seven months, Kim was slower than usual but feeling better since she had stopped the chemo. There was even talk that she was doing so well, she might have to go off hospice. But before they could deal with that issue, she suddenly became weaker. Her doctor said this was the cancer advancing.

Kim's world seemed to shrink as she was withdrawing more and more. Ryan was by her side every day, and they agreed that whatever the afterlife was, they would meet again. Kim was no longer getting out of bed and eventually lost consciousness. The hospice nurses were there more and more, and Ryan could see that his wife's body was no longer serving her. He would utter the same words to her that she used to say to him at the library where they first met: "Time to go." He would whisper in her ear, "I'll be all right. You go where you need to go, and we'll see each other again."

When Kim's body began to fail, however, Ryan's peaceful demeanor took a drastic turn. He began begging her, "Please don't leave me. You can't go. You must hang on."

Nevertheless, Kim died a few hours later.

A year and a half later, Ryan sat in his bereavement group and stated that he remains haunted. "The grief is unbearable because I screwed up so terribly. Kim and I agreed that when her time came, I would let her go, knowing I would see her again. But when she was actually dying, I panicked. I begged her not to go and broke our promise."

Ryan forgot that he is human—that life is precious, and he loved his wife dearly. Before her death, he could say, "When the time comes, I'll let you go," but when the moment became real, those were not his authentic words. He was feeling shame and blame for saying what was truly in his heart. He was feeling incredibly guilty and was sure that he had failed his wife.

The question was proposed to him in his group: "What if Kim was the one at your deathbed and said, 'Don't go'? Would you interpret that as her failing you, or would you see it as her loving you so much that she didn't want to say good-bye?"

The Universe translates our words through our intentions, lovingly and without judgment. The Universe didn't hear Ryan refusing to let go of his wife. It only heard his love for Kim even though he was repeating to himself, *I said those words and really screwed up.*

Ryan was able to work through his grief, and now whenever he feels bad about what happened, he sends loving thoughts to himself, such as:

*I could not say those words because
my love was too strong.*

If that doesn't help, Ryan repeats to himself:

*I could not let go because I loved Kim so much. Now that
she is gone, that love follows her wherever she might be.*

I now release her with all my love.

Grieving Around Birthdays, Anniversaries, and Holidays

Birthdays, anniversaries, and holidays often represent togetherness. But what happens when the people we love are no longer with us? These special days are some of the milestones of life that we all share with each other. While no one can change the physical reality of a loved one dying, how we hold the experience after a loss makes all the difference in the world.

Regina, a single mother, lavished her daughter, Connie, with affection. It had been just the two of them since Connie was five and her dad had left them both. Since Regina was a marketing consultant for a large banking chain, she was able to choose her hours, so she always made sure that she had time to be with her daughter.

In addition to Christmas and New Year's Eve, their favorite holidays to celebrate were their birthdays. Regina was born on January 19, and her daughter was born on March 16. Birthdays had not been a huge deal in Regina's life when she was growing up, so she wanted to make them an important reminder for Connie of how happy she was that she had been born.

When Connie was very little, Regina's friends attended the birthday parties. But once Connie was in school, she started inviting her own friends. One day, Connie asked her mother, "Why don't we celebrate your birthday?"

Regina said, "It's more of a kid thing."

"Isn't the day you were born important?" Connie shot back.

"Well yes, but—"

Connie interrupted, saying, "Your friends have birthday parties that you go to."

Regina realized that she didn't have a great explanation for not making a big deal out of her own birthday. After that, they had two parties a year, one for each of them. Connie loved it, and Regina thought, *I'll do this for a year or two, and it will pass. Birthday parties are a lot of work.*

But after a couple of years, Regina realized that she liked both celebrations.

Fast-forward 25 years. Connie was in her mid-30s, and Regina was in her mid-50s. Connie was married and had kids of her own. Regina lived about an hour away, where she had bought a small house in the suburbs. She fixed the house up and began running her small marketing/consulting business from there. One thing that remained constant in their lives was their dedication to celebrating their birthdays together.

Fast-forward another 15 years. The tradition was now reversed. Connie and her children, Regina's grandkids, made the trek every year to pick up a number of Regina's friends to celebrate her birthday. These parties were subdued because now that she was in her 70s, Regina preferred to have a simple dinner with coffee and cake for dessert.

On her 72nd birthday, Regina greeted her friends and family as usual. There was one new guest, a neighbor who had moved in next door, who remarked, "I've never seen a daughter make such a fuss over her mother's birthday."

Regina and Connie recounted the early days when Connie was a little girl and Regina a single mother. They explained how their birthday celebrations came to be.

But in the upcoming year, Regina began to feel weak and was often tired. She just didn't have any energy, and she had an upset stomach most of the time. After an intense workup by her doctor, she was diagnosed with gastric cancer.

In the beginning of March, Connie brought her mom to the hospital for a second round of chemo. During her treatment one day, Regina looked around the chemotherapy infusion room and said to her grown daughter, "Your birthday is coming up. I may not be able to make it."

"Don't be silly, Mom. I'll bring the birthday to you. I noticed the nursing station seats seven. Why don't we have it there?"

Regina replied, "I guess we could use the IV poles from the infusion room as a place to hang balloons." They both laughed.

Later that night, Connie discussed what to do about her upcoming birthday with her husband, Greg. He said, "She'll be discharged by then, and she would never want you to cancel your birthday celebration. If she gets tired early, I'll drive her home."

Regina began running a temperature, and they postponed her discharge from the hospital until they got the infection resolved. But they couldn't find the source of the infection, and in a few days, her condition worsened. The doctors explained that they had her on multiple antibiotics, and her body had gone septic. They were now afraid her breathing would become compromised.

After making a few calls, Connie told her husband, "Cancel my birthday get-together with my friends." She sat by her mother's bed each night, and other family members and friends stayed with Regina during the day. When she eventually lost consciousness, Connie remained with her mother around the clock. One day, when a visiting friend was leaving, she asked Connie if there was anything she could do.

"Thank you. Just your coming here was enough."

"Well, if I don't see you tomorrow," her friend said, "just know that I'm wishing you a happy birthday."

Connie was shocked to remember that tomorrow was in fact her birthday. "Oh, yes, I forgot," she replied. "I'll be where I always am, spending it with my mother."

She asked a friend to get a few balloons for tomorrow because she was sure Regina would wake up for the birthday. As calls came in and friends wanted to drop by, Connie decided to let her husband, kids, and a few close friends stop in throughout the day to wish her a happy birthday, still hoping that her mother would wake up.

By 3 p.m., she saw the nurse's activity levels increase around Regina, as they kept taking her vital signs over and over. Connie suddenly realized that her mom was taking a turn for the worse. Then the doctor walked in and said, "As you can tell, your mother isn't doing well, and we're going to be moving her to the ICU."

"I have to be with her."

"Yes, of course," the doctor replied.

After a couple of hours in the ICU, Connie realized that her mom might be dying soon. Then, without warning, the medical team rushed in and asked her to move away from her mother's side so they could start CPR. Regina's heart rate was dropping significantly, and within minutes, it was over. She had died.

Later, Connie was surprised when people said, "Oh my gosh. I'm so sorry that your mother died on your birthday," and "Your birthday was ruined. It's so sad that your mother's death will always be connected to your birthday." But Connie didn't view it in a negative light.

In the months that followed, she began to give some thought to everyone's negative interpretation of her mother dying on her birthday. Her husband asked, "Why do you see this so differently from everyone else?"

"People think that my mom and I weren't connected on my birthday, which is silly once you realize she gave birth to me on that day. It's almost like they have the impression that because she died on my birthday, I'm going to think of her sadly every year on that day. But I see it as a beautiful full-circle moment. She was with me the moment I took my first breath in this world, and I was with her the moment she took her last breath in the world. It was the most special birthday gift she could have ever given me."

How many of us put a negative interpretation on the day our loved one died? Do we talk about how a special day or holiday was forever ruined by their passing? Think of Connie's interpretation. Her mother's dying didn't ruin her birthday at all—on the contrary, it enriched it.

We have such a profound way of affecting our inner world by the words we choose. The word *ruined* versus *enriched* can make all the difference. So many of us might say, "I'll never have a good birthday again," or "That black cloud will always hover over my birthday from now on." Instead, Connie would think:

I remember my mother with love.

I celebrate my birthday with gratitude and love.

My birth and life were made possible by my mother.

*Today I celebrate my birth and my
mother who gave birth to me.*

❧ ❧ ❧

Anniversaries often take on a more painful meaning after loss and death. After loss, we add new anniversaries, such as the day our loved one died. Every symbol of the anniversary of a death matters to us: one month, six months, a year, and so on.

Adrian had always been at a loss for what to do on the anniversary of her mother's death. She tried keeping busy, she tried traveling . . . she tried doing everything under the sun to distract herself. But no matter what, she couldn't escape the pain. She eventually came to the conclusion that the only way out of the pain was through it. She decided that from then on, she would make an annual visit to her mother's grave.

For the next few years on the anniversary of her mother's death, Adrian would sit by her mother's graveside and cry, letting out all the sadness. She found it healing when her tears went down her face and landed on the earth below. This year, she was taken aback when she sat by her mother's grave and no tears came. She wondered what was wrong when it hit her: For the first time, she was remembering her mother from a place of love rather than pain. Because she had allowed herself to be free and fully grieve, she had arrived at a new, loving place. Now she could be grateful for her mother and the role she had played during her life.

Anniversaries can be a time to honor yourself for having strength and courage. They can be a day to honor your loved one. A year ago or many years ago, you were a different person, but life has changed. The person you were has forever changed. A part of the old you died with your loved one, but a part of your loved one lives on in the new you. This can be a holy transition instead of a lose-lose frame of mind.

Today, I honor my loved one.

On this anniversary, I remember my loved one with joy and gratitude.

❧ ❧ ❧

Holidays are about togetherness. When you've lost someone special, your world loses its celebratory qualities. Holidays only magnify loss, since the sadness feels sadder and the loneliness goes deeper. Many people feel that they're victims of their memories, but that doesn't have to be the case. You can take control of how you remember your loved one, and you can take control of how you *honor* him or her on a holiday.

For some, it makes sense to ignore the holidays as if they didn't exist. But for others, it makes sense to take control of them. You don't have to do them the way you always have in the past. Simply going through the motions without any meaning might seem pointless—and the worst loneliness of all.

After Marie's husband died, she and her daughters, like so many other families, tried to carry on. Luckily, Marie heeded her intuition and sensed when something wasn't working. She also knew that grief needed space.

"Holidays were so important to us as a family," she said, "and suddenly there was this huge void. Now every holiday is a bombardment, a hole that reminds us that he's not here. We tried to re-create the holidays and thought we could carry on as usual, but we learned quickly that we couldn't do it the way we did it before, not without my husband. It was just too hard and sad.

"The first Christmas we kind of glided through because we said, 'Okay, we're going to do this.' On the second Christmas, we put up the tree, but it took us a week to hang the decorations. We needed time to grieve without trying to be happy. We were all still so sad. Then we came to a mutual agreement to take a break from Christmas for a couple of years. We decided that when we came back to it again, we would start a new tradition."

Marie chose not to keep up the pretense of happiness when she and her children were mourning. She knew what was right for them, and she taught her daughters to honor their authentic feelings of not feeling celebratory. Marie even said that they actually felt closer by not doing the holidays. Then, after some healing time, Marie and her family were able to celebrate again, not the way they had before, but in new ways.

Instead of thinking, *Let's pretend this didn't happen, Everything is fine,* or *We're still going to have a great time even though we're sad,* she thought:

> *We find joy in each other without
> any pressure to be any other way.*

     ❧ ❧ ❧

You may find it difficult *not* to acknowledge a holiday, but you also don't want to pretend. You can integrate the loss into the holiday by giving it a time and place. Perhaps a prayer before dinner includes your loved one, or maybe you light a candle for him or her. A simple gesture of recognizing your loved one can reflect the everlasting love in your heart. Making time for your loss and acknowledging it is often a lot easier than resisting it.

You might think:

Even though this is our first Thanksgiving without our mother, we will say her name and remember her with love at our dinner table.

We light this candle in our sister's name and send her love.

Let's share a fond memory or a funny story about our loved one who lives on in our heart.

Your thinking may become negative, and you'll probably feel sad. That is normal and human. You may miss your loved one every day. You might feel lonely. Just pay attention to the thoughts you're holding and repeating. Repeating the negative ones can send you into a dark place that doesn't honor your loved one or yourself.

Sometimes our loved one's death may become linked to a certain holiday. Perhaps your husband died the day before Valentine's Day or on Mother's Day or Father's Day. You'll never forget that he died right after Easter or that that was his last Passover. Maybe he died on New Year's Eve or near the Fourth of July. From then on, these holidays will never be the same. Since holidays are markers, even if your loved one didn't die near a particular one, you may still look back and think that was his last Thanksgiving or his last Christmas. Some individuals knew it was their last holiday, and some didn't. Either way, a formerly joyous holiday is changed forever. The question is, does that day become a holiday that honors the memory of your loved one, or is it now just a recurring doomsday?

It's completely natural to think that you may *never* enjoy the holidays again. They will certainly never be the same as they were. However, in time, most people are able to find new meaning in the traditions of the holiday spirit that grow as a testament to love instead of loss.

Holidays are clearly some of the roughest terrain you navigate after a loss, and you can handle them as the individual you are. What is truly important is being present for the love reflected in the loss.

This holiday, we honor the love more than the loss.

Holidays are part of the journey to be felt fully. You can focus on the love and memories that you shared. And ultimately, you get to choose the content of your holiday experience.

Try to invite positive words in your interpretations. Words can grind you down or polish you up. The pain from grief can wound you, but positive thinking and kindness can heal you.

We remember you with our sweetest love today.

Responsibility and Blame

When death comes into our world, it's very common to try to find the reason that it occurred. We want to assign its visitation to a misdiagnosis, self-destructive behavior, or negligence because we have trouble making peace with the idea that death happens. Even in emergency rooms, after a car accident, you can hear health-care workers asking, "Was she wearing her seat belt?" When someone is admitted to the hospital for lung cancer, we ask, "Was she a smoker?" If we can find a reason why death visited our loved ones, maybe we can avoid doing what they did and death might just skip over us.

In the Western world, people almost believe that death is optional—but of course that's not how it works. To be born is to take part in an unwritten agreement that we will die someday. Where there is sun, there is shadow. Where there is life, there is death. There is a bit of arrogance in thinking that death will not visit us, or that somehow we can prevent it.

In the popular movie *Groundhog Day,* the main character, Phil, played by Bill Murray, relives the same day over and over again. By doing so, he is able to change the way he deals with the experiences in his life. The movie illustrates how the events may not change, but Phil can react to them in so many different ways that by the end, the day is completely transformed.

When he meets a homeless man who dies, Phil is determined to change his fate. When he relives the day, he tries to give the homeless man some money. Then he brings him to a restaurant and feeds him, but that doesn't change the inevitability of the man's death either. Despite all of Phil's interventions, the man dies anyway, and Phil realizes that however much control he has over his life, he cannot control death.

Yet many people really convince themselves that if they change what they do, they might not die. The point is not that eating right, exercising, or making healthy choices are useless because we're going to die anyway. Rather, we strive to eat well, exercise regularly, and make positive choices because that's the loving way to treat our bodies. When someone calls that a contradiction, we might say, "You should do all those things because they benefit your body." They'll likely add years to your life, but don't simply do them because you hope to escape death.

Remind yourself that you are responsible for your health, and you are not to blame for any illnesses you may get. It's helpful to look into cause and effect concerning an illness, but that doesn't mean you should blame yourself if you do become ill, or feel like you failed when you are dying.

Assigning Fault

Sometimes when bad things happen, our first instinct is to look for who is at fault.

Anita was a 19-year-old college student majoring in dance. Her dorm leader, Cathy, also studied dance, but in the graduate program. Anita loved Cathy, who was a bit of a housemother and very sweet—she always helped students with their disagreements and was a calming influence on everyone.

One day Anita was heading to her dorm room when she bumped into Cathy's boyfriend, Bert. "Hey, have you seen Cathy?" he asked her.

"Not today."

"If you run into her, let her know I'm at the coffee shop."

When Anita got to the common room in the dorm and saw Cathy, she passed on Bert's message.

"Thanks," Cathy said and went to meet him.

About an hour later, Anita heard that there had been a terrible car accident on the main road leading to the mall. It turns out that Cathy had been hit by a car and was killed instantly.

When Anita first heard about it, she was shocked and devastated. But as time went on, she realized that if she hadn't given Cathy the message, she would still be alive.

At the funeral, Anita thought about how she had played a part in her friend's death. No one had said so, but she felt it and talked to a few of her friends about it. One of them told her, "It wasn't your fault. You couldn't have known what was going to happen."

Another said, "You were just doing what Bert asked you to do. You were being nice."

Anita knew they were all telling her the truth, and yet she still felt responsible. She kept telling herself, *I should have kept my mouth shut.* Soon the sentence, *If I hadn't told her, Cathy would be alive,* played like a broken record in her mind.

Anita was very naïve at this point in her young life, and she believed that she had in fact played a significant role in her friend's death. *Before I entered the scene,* she thought, *everything was fine. I must be bad. My entering a situation makes it worse. I bring no good to anything.* She thought over and over, *I'm bad luck.*

Anita dropped out of school shortly after this and got involved in some horrible relationships. Her next

five years were a living hell. She lost contact with everyone she knew, as she moved from place to place, getting
fired, getting hired . . . doing whatever would earn her
some money.

One day, her travels took her back to the small uni-
versity town where it had all happened. As fate would
have it, she ran into Bert, who, after receiving his master's degree, had become a psychology professor at his
alma mater. Bert had no idea what had happened to
Anita, since people leave college all the time for many
reasons. But after they started talking, it was clear to
him that her life had really gone downhill.

"Anita, it wasn't your fault that Cathy died. If that's
your thinking, then it was *my* fault for asking you to give
her the message. I would never have done anything to
deliberately cause her death."

"Of course not," said Anita. "I know how much you
loved her, so why would anyone think it was your fault?"

"Why is that true for me, but not true for you?"

Anita suddenly realized what she had done to herself. She and Bert became close friends from that point
on, and he did his best over time to help her see how her
thinking had been her downfall, not Cathy dying.

Eventually, Anita came to believe it, and she shared
Bert's words with others. Coming from him, since he
was practically in the same situation as she was, made
all the difference. Her awareness of her thinking was
the key. She had turned her grief into blame and onto
herself.

In the blame game, no one wins, no one is at peace.
Our loved ones would never want their death to ruin our
life. A death reminds us of the love we have to give and

the life we have left. It is a gift to use our remaining time well in honor of our loved ones who died.

If we were truly and absolutely responsible for another person's life and death, we would have chosen life for them. Think about Anita and Cathy. If Anita were actually given a choice, she would of course have chosen for Cathy to be alive, but the fact that Cathy died means that it was not within Anita's control.

My life is the only one I am responsible for.

My life is a gift.

I free myself from all guilt and judgment.

Releasing Negative Interpretations

Jack said good-bye to everyone at work, excited that he was taking off for a week to go on a cruise with his wife. He promised his co-workers that he would not spend a moment of his vacation thinking about his job. They knew this would be a huge accomplishment for him because as a general manager of a popular hotel chain, he had not taken any vacation time for many years.

While Jack was gone, his co-workers hoped he was enjoying himself on the cruise and not assessing the presentation of meals, efficiency of housekeeping, or front-desk operations. Three days before he was scheduled to return, things had run pretty well without him—his presence had clearly been missed, but everyone was proud of the work they had done in his absence.

Then the call came. Jack had had a massive heart attack on the ship and died instantly. His co-workers spent the next few days trying to digest the news and found themselves sitting in front of an employee-assistance counselor whom their corporate headquarters had sent in. The things they were saying were very revealing as to how they were processing grief in respect to the given situation.

The head of food services, Jim, said, "I'll never go on a vacation." He elaborated, "Seriously, the guy never took time off. He finally goes away, and what happens? He dies."

Jeanette, the head of housekeeping, said, "Life sucks. You try to take care of yourself and enjoy life, and something like this happens."

Julie, another manager, remarked, "Jack was such a nice guy, always trying to do the right thing, and he died before he even reached the age to write his bucket list."

All of these statements are negative interpretations. We may feel that someone died too soon, and we may never be able to understand the "whys" of it. But what do those negative interpretations do to our own lives? What if each life is here to teach the rest of us lessons? What if each death holds a lesson, too? Can we look back on Jack's life and find the lessons? His co-workers would say that he loved his work. Can we say:

It is great that Jack did what he wanted to do in life.

If we judge him, which is really a judgment of ourselves, we can see that he didn't take as much time to enjoy life, so we could affirm:

Jack's life and death are reminders to live a balanced life.

Another lesson we can learn from Jack is to take the time to ask ourselves important questions:

- *Am I living the life I want?*

- *If I died tomorrow, would I die with regrets?*

- *Is this really how I want to be spending my days?*

- *What positive changes could I make in my life while I have the time to implement them?*

When we examine the aspect of responsibility and blame, Jack's life and death remind all of us to live in balance. To his co-workers, his death can either be interpreted as a message of blame or a wake-up call to negative thought patterns. They were reminded of their clear choice between "Why bother with a vacation? You're just going to die anyway," and "My life is a gift. I want to fully embrace my work life, and I want to fully embrace my vacations."

Jack's example is to remind us to live the lives we were meant to have, and that also means allowing time for grieving. What would grief look like if we just let the feelings go through us? What if we felt them and allowed sadness to wash over us like a spring rain, and then moved on to the next feeling? This doesn't mean that our memories or our love for those who have died moves on; rather, we've come to a place where we have a warm spot in our heart for them, always.

Honoring Your Grief

When we come to the realization that we're not responsible for our loved one's death, we are left with the question, "What are we responsible for?" Of course the obvious answer is that we're responsible for our own life, which means we're responsible for our own grief as well. How do we take responsibility for our grief? We honor it. An interesting lesson can be learned from Martha, a hospice nurse.

Martha attended a patient's funeral that was held in the hospital chapel. Her new boss, Alisha, arrived toward the end of the service and was surprised to see Martha sobbing quietly from her gut. She was concerned that the nurse seemed so devastated by a patient's death and thought to herself, *I might need to send Martha home. Maybe she isn't cut out for hospice work.*

When it was over, Alisha walked up to Martha and asked her if she was okay.

"Yes," Martha replied as she composed herself.

"I'm concerned about you," Alisha said. "I know you've been taking care of this patient for a long time, but you seem really distraught. Are you able to go back to work?"

"Yes, I am," Martha said. "When a patient dies, I allow myself to feel all the sorrow. Then I can go back to work. I want to feel all my feelings instead of carrying them into the next moment or to the next patient."

That nurse had a great point. We often think that if we allow all our feelings of sorrow to come out, we'll be overwhelmed. And of course we find that one loss triggers an older loss from the past that we didn't fully grieve. How would our lives look if we allowed ourselves to fully grieve each and every loss? Then we could truly be in the moment and move to the next feeling that comes up in life. There would be a lot less suffering in the world if we honored our grief, but not the sorrow.

Grief is real because loss is real. Each period of grief has its own imprint, as distinctive and unique as the person who was lost. We think we want to avoid grief, but really it's the pain of the loss that we want to avoid. Grief is the healing process that ultimately brings us comfort in our pain if we allow it to happen without the interference of our distorted thinking.

Rising Above Grief

When you rise above your initial thoughts about grief, you can find gratitude for the time you and your loved one shared together, as short as that seems to have been. It's possible to discover so many hidden gifts.

In grief, it's hard to imagine that anything good can come out of a loss. And it's important when consoling someone who's grieving to not try to point out the silver lining. When you've lost someone you love dearly, there is no silver lining to be found. What does exist is that in accepting the loss over time, you may also find a deeper meaning. That meaning is often called the "sixth stage" when we're referring to Kübler-Ross's Five Stages of Grief (which, as a reminder, are *denial, anger, bargaining, depression,* and *acceptance.*)

This can take many forms, but at its heart, it is an affirmation in itself. A tragedy happened, but the affirmation behind the change that people take on is something like:

I am not a victim of this tragedy.

I will grow from this experience.

A good example of growth through loss and rising above grief is from Candy Lightner, who founded the organization Mothers Against Drunk Driving (MADD) when her 13-year-old daughter was killed by a drunk driver. Candy had every right to be bitter and become a victim of her circumstances. Even though it was a tragic accident and no one would have denied her a pity party, she made a different choice. She dedicated her life to raising awareness and passing stricter laws to help prevent drinking and driving, and protecting people from needlessly dying at the hands of drunk drivers.

When we release blame and take responsibility, there is greatness to be found. That greatness is the power of grief. We don't always recognize its healing powers, yet they are extraordinary. It is just as amazing as the physical healing that occurs after a car accident or major surgery. Grief changes and re-creates a devastated life. It heals a wounded soul.

Recall a time when someone close to you experienced a significant loss, and think of that person's life following the loss. Then think of him or her a year later. Then two years later. If the individual released the blame and guilt and took responsibility for their grief, a miraculous shift would occur. If a healing doesn't take place, it's most likely because the person's negative thinking is making too much noise for true healing to occur. Here are some positive thoughts to keep in mind:

Grief mixed with love always works.

Grief mixed with love always heals.

Coping with Suicide

Suicide can be one of the hardest losses you will ever deal with. In the aftermath of suicide, there are some key points to think about. Your loved one who committed suicide was not "bad." His or her soul was in tremendous pain. For reasons beyond your knowing, that soul chose to leave this incarnation.

While you may believe that there are things you could have done and missed, you must find that place to trust that there is an all-knowing and all-loving Universe that is always watching over your soul and its growth. If your thinking or beliefs tell you that a loved one's suicide was a horrible mistake, know that spiritually the Universe oversees all souls and their trajectories. The Universe has never lost, forgotten, or misplaced a soul.

Derrick had worked at a suicide-prevention hotline for ten years. It wasn't a paid job; it was done on a volunteer basis. During the day, he was an accountant for a large accounting firm and would often get asked, "How do you stand working at a suicide hotline? What do you do when you can't save someone?"

Derrick would always reply, "My grandmother used to have a saying: 'If everyone swept in front of their own door, the world would be a cleaner place.'" He explained that his grandmother's words were about not being a busybody, and taking care of what was in front of you. "I expanded that in my own life," he said, "and in my work on the hotline. I think about my interactions, my reactions, and what I'm putting out in the world as what's in front of my door. It's the only world I have control over. What someone else does or thinks is what's in front of their door. It's never my place to go over there and start messing around.

"There are only three areas: my front door, your front door, and God's front door. All I can do is focus on sweeping in front of my *own* door: being loving, respectful, and understanding, and always showing kindness and compassion to callers. What others do with that information is their business. Who lives and who dies is God's business—that's at His front door."

When it comes to suicide, there is no right or wrong time. There is just *our* time. It was our time to be born and our time to go. In these moments, you need to be sure that you are still loving yourself. Do not lose faith, because you are a beautiful human being who deserves to be loved despite the circumstances you find yourself in.

What you need to look at is what you do with your thoughts and feelings. If you find your mind going to another person's struggles, you may want to remember that in death, your loved one is no longer in that deep anguish. Some helpful affirmations include:

My loved one is no longer in pain.

My loved one's soul is now released and free.

In terms of your loss, it's not unusual to feel guilt over what you perceive may have been your part in your loved one's suicide. Perhaps you think you missed a signal or a warning. If so, practice these affirmations:

I give all my guilt to my higher power.

I recognize that [insert name of your loved one] *soul's journey is happening exactly as it was meant to be.*

You may feel angry that your loved one did this to you, but you are not a victim of the suicide. Whatever the circumstances may be, this person's death wasn't something "done" to you. It's sometimes helpful to remember the truth about relationships and acknowledge what you can and can't control. A couple of affirmations may be:

I release my anger and ask God for healing.

Our souls are joined forever beyond this earthly plane.

It's vital to remember that the love you shared cannot be harmed or touched or damaged by one person's death. Someday your soul will understand the awareness that how you die in this lifetime is only one small part of the story.

This type of death often calls for lots of forgiveness:

I forgive my loved one for leaving.

*I forgive my loved one for everything that
I perceive he or she did in this lifetime.*

Recognize that your loved one's body and mind were lost and in pain. Try if you can to meet that pain with love and compassion, knowing that in this lifetime, there were some dragons that this person simply couldn't slay. Then take that same love and compassion and apply it to your own thoughts and actions:

I forgive myself for everything I think I did not do.

*I forgive myself for everything I did
that I judged I should not have done.*

I forgive myself completely for everything.

I recognize that only the love is real.

While it is important to heal the guilt about your actions or your judgment of your lack of actions, the guilt is a reflection of your behavior, while shame may be a statement of who you think you are. There are a lot of internal messages following a suicide, such as, *I wasn't worth staying around for. My life didn't matter to my loved one. Our marriage, our family, and our world was so screwed up, that my loved one would rather die than be in it.* None of these statements reflects the truth about who you are. Instead, try these:

I recognize my own worth.

I am lovable no matter what happens in the world.

My soul's worth is always of value.

My relationships are sacred.

In the end, what is most important is that you realize that you cannot be responsible for someone else's death. No one has the ability to know what each soul's lessons are. There is no way you can predict what journey any soul is supposed to take in this lifetime. You can only come back to what you know in your mind and heart is true:

I am responsible for my own soul's journey.

Healing Following a Child's Death

It's been said that losing a child is one of the most catastrophic traumas an individual can endure. How does a parent fully grieve and find healing after such a loss? Part of parenting is being responsible for another person's life, so how can we ask parents to release their feelings of guilt or blame when tragedy strikes? Does it seem insensitive or heartless to even suggest it?

The death of a child is an example of when healing is not only a way to honor the loss, but it is also vital for the surviving family members. As in the earlier example of Candy Lightner, we witnessed the amazing power of grief and the gifts it can offer us. Even after losing her beloved daughter, Candy became a shining example of rising above grief to not only heal herself, but to also positively impact the lives of countless others. Once again, the best way to illustrate the tremendous healing potential of grief is through a story, and we were fortunate to come upon a very powerful one. We decided to leave it in the voice of the author, who happens to be a mother:

> The last day of my son's life started out like any other. After our morning ritual of singing a wake-up

song, tickling, and getting dressed, I walked my son Jesse, who was six years old, outside to meet his father, who was picking him up for school. Jesse's 12-year-old brother, JT, had already left on the bus.

I was in a hurry to get to work, but as I gave Jesse a hug good-bye, I noticed that he had written in the frost on my car's window. The message he wrote said, "I love you," along with three hearts carefully drawn with his little finger. My heart melted, and I made the conscious decision to run back into the house to get my phone so that I could take a picture of it. It was a chilly December morning, but the sun was bright, and I posed Jesse in front of his loving message and angled the camera as best I could to capture both him and his message. Then he was on his way, and this was the very last time I would see my son alive.

Jesse was a first grader at Sandy Hook Elementary School. That morning, which was December 14, 2012, a mentally ill young man shot out the front entrance of the school and walked into the building. He gunned down my precious Jesse and 19 other students, along with six teachers and administrators. I was later informed that Jesse died while bravely running into harm's way in an attempt to save his classmates. Although I was told this later, I already knew in my heart that this was what Jesse would have done; in his courageous, selfless way, he would have thought he could save the day.

I spoke at Jesse's funeral, standing just behind his small white casket. Afterward, many people kept asking me what they could do. This whole tragedy started with an angry thought, so my advice to people was to change an angry thought into a loving one, each and every day. After all, it is only a choice. Start with one thought a day, and I believe we can make this a more loving place. Over time, my friends and even strangers have continued to reach out to me to tell me how this message has positively changed their lives, and how they're now spreading the word to their own families and friends. It's just a simple choice, but it's powerful enough to change lives, and maybe even the world.

To honor Jesse's memory and enable myself to continue on, I made a conscious decision to face this senseless tragedy with love and forgiveness. The outpouring of love and support from our town, the nation, and the entire world has shown that we *can* unite as one in love and be victorious in the face of evil. I believe this tragedy has changed many lives for the better, as individuals are now choosing a more loving, compassionate path.

We are all faced with a choice when we wake up in the morning: Will we choose to live our lives in fear or in faith? Then we step out into the world where good and evil do battle every day. It is the charge of each one of us to bring light and love into the world, and we achieve this through every thought and interaction we have on a daily basis.

Regardless of the circumstances, death is one of the hardest experiences we human beings go through on our journey here on Earth. Despite the pain, we can see that there are other ways to think about and honor our loved ones. For example, as we discussed earlier, we need to remember that birthdays, anniversaries, and other holidays can become reminders that our love is eternal.

When you're having a hard time with your grief or struggling to hold on to the connection with your loved one, try this exercise:

Find a quiet place to sit with no distractions. Close your eyes, and focus on your breathing, slowing down each inhale and exhale.

Picture your loved one's face in your mind's eye. See her at a happy time in her life.

Allow her essence to fill your inner space. See her eyes sparkle, the glow of her face. Feel the connection between the two of you that continues. Now tell your loved one anything that you need to say. If you feel it in your heart, she will feel it in hers. Understand that this connection remains unbroken even though she is no longer in her body.

Now listen in the quietness for anything that she may want to say to you. After you have heard what she has to say, if anything, thank her for the connection that remains and breathe it into your heart. Release all the strings that attach you except the one delicate string that flows from heart to heart.

When you're ready, bring your awareness back to your breath, open your eyes, and ground yourself in your body. When you stand up and walk away, remember that your loved one walks with you. The ultimate truth is that love never dies.

If anything negative came up for you during this exercise, treat it as a gift of knowledge. Do you need to forgive your loved one? Does he or she need to forgive you? Did you get in touch with any blame or guilt you're holding on to? If so, remember that embracing your grief can help you heal.

❧ ❧ ❧

As you allow yourself to fully feel your grief, begin to release the negative thought patterns around blame and guilt. No matter how a loved one died, know that you can in time find sweet gratitude that you shared part of each other's journey together. Ultimately, you'll realize the truth: The power of love cannot be knocked down by death.

In the next chapter, we'll look at another type of loss that deeply affects us—the death of a beloved pet—and apply the same tools of grieving and forgiveness so that we can both heal ourselves and honor and acknowledge a profound loss.

∼

CHAPTER FIVE

HONORING
PET LOSS

Grief is a natural reflection of life and exists in any relationship where we have feelings and attachments. We all mourn for those we loved, for those we disliked, and even for those we hated. We don't grieve when there is no attachment. In that context, it seems silly to think that we wouldn't grieve for the animals in our life that we are indeed very much attached to.

Our pets share our living spaces—and in many cases, our beds—and are truly members of the family. Despite this, people who are grieving over an animal that died will often find that they must be very discreet about their feelings and with whom they share them. They instinctively know that they're dealing with a form of disenfranchised grief—a type of grief that other people might deem as "less than." Some have shared their heartbreak only to be met with: "Well, it's not like it was a person. It was just an animal," and "Just go get yourself another pet."

The reality is that grief from pet loss is not as easily fixed as some would have us believe. It's hard to live in grief that's judged as unworthy. Grief is about love, and our animal companions often show us some of the most unconditional love we could ever experience. How often, despite our best efforts, do we absorb some of society's judgments and think, *I shouldn't be grieving this much?* Yet when we let these thoughts in, we betray our genuine feelings.

To complicate our grief even more around pet loss, we're often clearer on treating them humanely. When they're in pain at the end of their lives, despite our wanting them to stay around, we will often choose to euthanize them to make sure that they die in a respectful, dignified manner, surrounded by love. But sometimes it makes the loss a little harder when we wonder if we did the right thing at the right time.

People feel very strongly about their animals. Many people resonate with humorist Will Rogers's statement: "If there are no dogs in heaven, then when I die, I want to go where they went."

Holding Pet Grief Preciously

Ella had a German shepherd named Garlic. He earned that name because despite Ella's best efforts, he always had bad breath. When people met him for the first time, they would comment on what a beautiful dog he was and that his breath wasn't really that bad. For years, Garlic was a fixture in the neighborhood. Whenever anyone was out and about, they couldn't help but greet the dog with a "Hey, Garlic!" whenever he was in the front yard or on a walk.

When Garlic died of old age, Ella and her family thought about how they had shared his life with the whole neighborhood, so why shouldn't they share his death with everyone, too? The alternative—that he would just disappear from the neighborhood like a child's toy or a patio chair—was unthinkable. And if they kept their grief private, they would be followed by weeks and months of randomly running into neighbors who would unknowingly ask, "Where's Garlic?" Then they'd have to explain it over and over again.

Ella decided to write an obituary for Garlic and e-mail it, along with a photo, to all of their neighbors. She used the list from the neighborhood-watch committee, although she was a bit concerned that there might be some backlash for using the list for that purpose. But her family affirmed the following to themselves:

We lovingly share our grief with our neighbors.

To their surprise, almost everyone received the news lovingly as well. And when Ella was in her neighbor's kitchen one day, there was Garlic's picture taped to their refrigerator. Ella and her family were also amazed by the number of e-mail responses they got back. One of them read: "You don't know us, but we knew Garlic. Garlic would visit our house every day around 4 when we brought the kids home from school. We often thought that such a sweet dog must have sweet owners. We hope to meet you soon and offer our sympathies in person."

Whenever Ella was asked about the obituary, she simply said, "His life mattered. Why shouldn't his death?" This was an amazing example of how she held her family's grief so preciously, that others in turn held the grief respectfully, too.

It's obvious that the neighborhood was changed by this dog's death. One person brought over a casserole, another brought a pie . . . just as if Garlic were a person. Someone else made a donation to a pet charity in his name. A profound sense of sweetness and tenderness blanketed the neighborhood and lasted long after Garlic's passing.

❧ ❧ ❧

There is a unique difficulty with the loss of pets as opposed to that of human loved ones. When we get a pet, we are automatically their caregivers for life. Like children, we take care of them, keep them safe, feed them, and tend to their well-being. They are our responsibility. This makes it easy to turn grief into guilt, believing that their death was our fault. The reality is that despite our best efforts to do everything for our pets, they will still die someday. This next story is a great demonstration of turning grief into guilt.

It was a Wednesday when Cheryl called her beloved cat, Timmy, while shaking his treat box, to come home for dinner. When he came up the stairs, Cheryl noticed that he wasn't walking right and seemed to be in pain. Her husband called around to find a veterinary clinic that was open all night, but the search was unsuccessful. Cheryl and her husband decided to stay by Timmy's side until morning.

The next morning they visited their vet, who ran some tests and found that Timmy had a urinary blockage. He said that he'd need to keep Timmy overnight, but Cheryl and her husband were welcome to call for updates to see how he was doing. They felt very relieved.

In the afternoon, Cheryl decided to take her seven-year-old daughter to the local pool and spend time with some friends. They had a wonderful afternoon, and on the way home, she decided to call the vet's office to see how Timmy was coming along. She had to pull over to the side of the road when she heard that Timmy had passed away just 20 minutes ago. It seems that the vet had left a message at her home, rather than on her cell phone.

Cheryl was shocked and immediately became filled with negative thoughts and reactions. She didn't know how she managed to drive the rest of the way home, but when she was back in the house, she broke down. "How could this have happened?" she moaned over and over. Apparently, Timmy's little heart just gave out, and Cheryl and the rest of the family were left shattered. Timmy was more than a cat to them. He had been their fellow family member and friend.

The guilt and questions that sometimes accompany grief set in almost immediately: *We should have driven around to find a clinic in the middle of the night. Why didn't we? Was it his diet that killed him? Did we feed him the wrong food? Did he have a delayed reaction to the Christmas ham we gave him as a treat? Was there too much salt in it? Why didn't we notice that he was drinking more water? How could I have been relaxing by the pool while Timmy was dying?*

They buried Timmy in front of a tree in the back-yard, and Cheryl would go out there and meditate. One afternoon, she began to talk to her beloved cat, telling him how sorry she was that she didn't do more to save him. She recalled, "I took a few deep breaths, and suddenly I felt a sense of calm overtaking me. Then I heard the words, 'Forgive yourself. You didn't do anything wrong. I know how much you loved me, and I am still around in spirit.' At first I thought I was making it up, but if I was, why did I feel so much more peaceful than I had since Timmy died? I believe he was helping me let go of the guilt and anger I was projecting onto myself."

After Cheryl received the message from Timmy, she said, "The grief I was feeling was actually a blessing, although I didn't realize it at the time. I had lost sight of the meaning in life and was taking my loved ones for granted! I had forgotten how precious life is. Grief was bringing us all closer together and bonding us even tighter. I'd been given a gift of unconditional love from one heart to another. That is the most important love in life, so we must hold our loved ones closer and love unconditionally, as we did our beloved Timmy!"

She added positive affirmations such as:

I forgive myself and set us both free.

I choose to focus on the blessing Timmy gave us of unconditional love.

After a few days, Cheryl started to feel lighter. She learned that this special cat will forever be a part of her heart, and knew that they would meet again in heaven.

Paying attention to our thinking is just as important with the loss of a pet as it is with the loss of a person. We use affirmations to remind ourselves of our goodness, our true identity—which, by the way, our pets always see in us. That is what makes their love unconditional. In grief, we can go back and look at why we didn't notice that our cat was drinking too much water or how stupid we were to give them an unhealthy treat. It's important to remember that our pets often get treats, and they don't die. Likewise, there are days when they're thirsty, and they don't die. As we go back and pick out things that caused their death, with our distorted thinking, it is nothing more than gathering evidence that we are "bad."

Timmy reminded Cheryl of the truth:

Forgive yourself. You did not do anything wrong. I know how much you loved me, and I am still around in spirit.

🐾 🐾 🐾

When we have relationships with people, they are only with us for a period of time. We don't know whether that's a month, a few years, or 50 years. The same is true with our pets. Perhaps one of the startling differences is that sometimes our pets will have a sense of when their life is winding down. We've all heard stories of when dogs or cats become ill and withdraw and isolate themselves until it's their time. What if pets also had a sense of when their death might be coming, even from an accident? The following story of Homer the dog is just such an example.

Homer had brown and black short hair on his lean body, and huge brown eyes that seemed to respond to every emotion around him. His owner, Andy, remembered the day his world changed.

"One Friday," Andy said, "my beloved Homer, whom I'd had for almost ten years, was hit and killed by a car in front of our house. He must not have seen it, as he was very good with the road and avoiding any cars. My wife and I were devastated. I meditate, as well as practice affirmations and mirror work daily, and I'd been having a feeling that Homer was going to be leaving. But I was preparing myself for a long, slow decline, not a sudden departure.

"On Sunday afternoon, after not being able to go more than 20 minutes without crying since it happened, I reached out to someone I knew who was an animal communicator. She told me that she connected with Homer, who said that he had tried to tell me he would be leaving, but I didn't want to believe it. He said the car was just the story around his departure—he was going to leave by some means or another.

"Homer also said that he had supported me long enough. I had journaled as much that morning. I had battled depression and negative thoughts for much of my life, and often he was the only one who heard my cries. I knew he had fulfilled his mission to help me, as I was no longer in such a painful place, and he had more work to do. I felt so amazingly blessed, and I didn't shed a tear the rest of the day. I could look at his toys, the yard, anywhere that he had spent time, and feel the joy that was there, not the sorrow."

Andy also received an outpouring of wonderful comments on his Facebook page and personal messages.

"I thought Facebook love was powerful on birthdays," Andy said, "but that has nothing on posting about a pet's death. Homer touched so many more lives than I ever imagined. And he continues to do so."

Besides fully embracing the grief that we feel when our pets die, just like humans, they often leave behind incredible lessons. Andy had cried in his sleep nightly, and one night before bed, anticipating another night of sadness and grief, he repeated to himself:

I will remember all the gifts that Homer gave me.

With that, he decided to write down all the affirming lessons he learned from his beloved dog. We believe that they apply not only to Homer, but oftentimes to all of us as well.

Lessons from Homer

I will live in the present moment.

The present moment is all that matters, and dogs are the perfect teachers of this. Homer would jump off the bed each morning, ready and eager for the day. He never held a grudge or was stuck in the past. He greeted every moment like it was a long lost friend.

I treat each experience as if it were the first time.

Homer met each meal, each treat, each walk, and each person with such vigor, excitement, and joy. His energy and enthusiasm were infectious. Everything was a celebration. Homer had a lust for life.

I ask for what I want.

Homer was a master manifester. He would sit, stare, beg, drool . . . whatever it took to get what he wanted. It never failed to work. His perseverance and tenacity were amazing. People always gave in and offered him a treat, pet him, or played ball with him.

I give and receive unconditional love.

Give and receive love. Be a conduit of love. Homer enjoyed other dogs, but he really loved people. He lived to sniff, snort, and smell people; and nothing made his eyes light up like being petted by a stranger when he was out for a walk.

I don't judge others or myself.

Don't judge yourself or others. Most of the time, Homer was a true Zen master—so sweet, easygoing, and relaxed. He accepted everyone and never wanted anyone to change.

Many believe that when we die, we will reunite with all of the people and pets we loved that passed on before us. We embrace the concept that death is arriving into fullness rather than emptiness. In other words, when any of us leaves the earthly plane, it will be "standing room only" because we will once again be surrounded by all of our loved ones whom we've been missing so much.

Let's imagine that scene with our pets greeting us as well. To see their faces again, their tails wagging. Hearing their barks, their meows, their chirps, their whinnies and grunts, and being around all of their other loving attributes. What a tender arrival we will have when we die.

I embrace all the gifts my pet has left me.

I am thankful for all the experiences we shared.

My sweet pet will always be surrounded by my love.

~

CHAPTER SIX

OTHER LOVES,
OTHER LOSSES

Besides breakups, divorce, and death, there are many other kinds of losses; and some are more obvious than others. Some we can easily identify, such as suffering a miscarriage or losing a job. Other losses are not so easy to see, such as not attaining the idealized career, mate, or even body type. We have to grieve what has been lost, but at other times we must also grieve what never was or will never be.

For many people, these losses have been with them for much of their lives, and all types of grief are worth examining and healing. For example, we want to bring a loss like miscarriage to light and recognize it as a signifi-cant event to grieve, as it's a genuine loss that deserves time and healing. The losses that are harder to see often stay in the background, thus providing a steady stream of misery.

When you allow the healing powers of grief to work, you may run across some of your own hard-to-see losses, so let's shine a light on them and allow a deeper healing to occur.

Infertility and Miscarriage

There are certain things in life that we often take for granted. For example, when little girls play house with their dolls, they assume that when they grow up, they'll be able to have a baby if they want to. They never imagine that their body's biological clock may wind down, that they may not be able to get pregnant, or that a pregnancy might not be successful. Nor would they be able to anticipate the amount of shame and stigma that some people attach to those things. If a woman wants a biological child but isn't able to conceive, she may feel that she isn't fulfilling her destiny as a female, or that she's letting down her partner. She will most likely not be able to predict the personal grief that accompanies the loss of that kind of attachment.

From a very young age, Jane knew that she would be a great mother one day. Many years later, she met a wonderful man named Donald. During their courtship, they did the usual exploration of "Do you want to have kids?" and discovered that they were both family oriented.

After a few years of marriage, Jane and Donald decided it was time to start their family, but after three months, she was surprised that she hadn't gotten pregnant. She decided to give it a few more months and if nothing happened, she would talk to her doctor. The months came and went, and she decided to make an appointment and not tell Donald about it.

Her doctor did some testing, and the results weren't encouraging. When Jane told Donald what was going on, he also got tested but learned that he was fine. And so, she decided to begin infertility treatments while at the same time subconsciously beginning a bout of negative self-talk. *I'm defective; something's wrong with me* ran though her mind like bad background music. Her husband seemed unfazed by the whole thing, but Jane was taking it hard.

A month later, on March 4, it was her birthday. Donald gave her a beautiful ring with the date on it, but they realized that the engraver transposed the day and month, so it said "4/3" rather than "3/4." Jane loved it but did plan to bring it back to have the date fixed. However, she never made it in because there was a bigger event in her future.

She was thrilled when she found out she was pregnant. Finally, her world was right again, and a baby was on its way. Unfortunately, that was not her destiny, and her pregnancy ended in a miscarriage. She felt completely devastated, broken and overwhelmed by sadness. Donald was supportive and mentioned that they could always adopt. He was the optimist of the pair with his "there are always other options" philosophy.

Jane didn't realize it at the time, but there was a lot more work to be done. Her mother intuited this, saying, "You need to take some time to really, fully grieve the unborn child you lost." In her despair, Jane realized that her mom was right. She had experienced more than a technical setback in her quest to have a child. It was a loss that needed to be grieved and healed.

As Jane took the time to feel the sadness, she told herself:

I honor the loss of my unborn child.

Everything is unfolding in the way it was meant to happen.

Donald remained open to adoption, but Jane wasn't quite ready. She needed to do more listening to what her self-talk was saying: *My body is broken. I can't be a real mother.* The more she listened to what her mind was telling her, the more she became aware of her distorted thinking and how cruelly she'd been talking to herself. She realized that she needed to change her thinking immediately and began reciting the following affirmations:

I forgive my body.

My body is doing everything it is destined to do.

All is well in my body.

My body is leading me to the perfect situation for the highest good of all involved.

In regard to being a mother, she said:

I am worthy of being a mother.

A real mother is defined by her ability to love.

Within a year, Jane made peace with everything, and she and Donald were well into the adoption process. They eventually brought home a beautiful little girl named Diana, and were shocked to learn that Diana's birthday was April 3, the date engraved on the ring that Jane always wore and never got around to fixing. Jane now feels that Diana came into her world as a miracle.

Jane realized that if her prayers had been answered or if she had birthed a child, she would not have met the wonderful being who is now her daughter. As she said, "Now I see that Diana was my destiny, as was infertility." She recognized the true essence of motherhood and the importance of forgiving her body, and she also knew that she had to allow herself to go through the grieving process.

Jane's story had a happy ending. One of the lessons she learned is that she needed to recognize and honor her grief. When it comes to infertility and miscarriage, other people may not give such grief its full due. Even those closest to the woman, such as her spouse or parents, might not comprehend the impact that such losses have on her. No one on the outside can possibly know the depth of a mother's pain, just as she cannot possibly know who she is destined to love in this world. It may be a child that she births or, like in Jane's example, a child she adopts as her own.

❧ ❧ ❧

Many women have said that when they reached menopause, grief began to show up, such as the grief that they will never be able to have a child or even have more children. Some mistakenly think their womanhood has been diminished. Whatever the change in your life may be, you must make sure to look within to honor your losses, feel the grief fully, and not attach negative thinking to it. Consider these affirmations:

As my body changes, my womanhood expands.

My life is an incredible journey of love and learning.

You'll ultimately learn the truth that who you are is beyond the circumstances of your life. Your essence is grander than anything going on with your body. You are an amazing being whether or not you have children. You are incredible during your child-rearing years and just as wonderful after them.

> *I am becoming a more beautiful,*
> *amazing woman every day.*

Job Loss

When it comes to types of losses, a big one for many people is job loss. This probably comes as no surprise because we live in a world that confuses "doing" with "being." In other words, what we do gets misinterpreted as who we are. When we meet someone new, one of the first questions we ask one another is: "What do you do?" So much value is placed on what we do for a living that when it's stripped away, we're left to wonder, *Who am I now?*

In 2008, Danny was having a regular morning working in the corporate office of a medical-equipment company, returning calls as usual. He had been with the same company for 30 years, so most of the day-to-day issues he encountered, he had already solved dozens of times. His work was now a well-worn path, and his office was his second home.

That afternoon, Danny had his monthly meeting with his boss, Keith. As he walked in with the usual files in hand, he noticed that Linda, the head of Human Resources, was sitting beside Keith. Keith then stood up and said, "I'll just step out for a bit and let you two talk." Danny thought nothing of this. He had met with HR many times before over the years due to various employee issues. Today, he wondered who had done what.

He was surprised when Linda said, "This is going to be a hard meeting, Danny."

Wow, he thought, *one of my employees must have done something really bad.*

He definitely wasn't prepared when she told him, "I'm sorry, but we have to let you go. Given the last few mergers, the CEO and executive team feel that we have enough talent, and your services have become redundant."

Danny sat there stunned as she continued. "We'll be keeping you on for two more weeks and then paying you three months of severance."

"Is this for sure?" Danny asked. "Can I talk to Keith about this? Maybe he'll change his mind."

Linda put her hand on his and said, "We both know that when he's made up his mind to do something, it's unchangeable. Just accept it, Danny."

For the next two weeks, Danny drove the commute that he had done repeatedly for the last 30 years, knowing that in a matter of days, he would never do it again. On his final day in the office, he packed up his belongings and looked around the room, realizing that he would never inhabit that space again. Three decades were ending in the amount of time he used to take for a vacation.

Luckily, his wife, Melissa, had been practicing affirmations for many years. She talked to him about accepting the loss, but not accepting his negative beliefs about it. They focused on the positive, and used the following affirmations:

My talents and abilities are in demand.

All is well.

I am safe.

"We need to be careful to watch our thoughts and spoken words," Melissa told him. "It takes a lot of effort, because we've both been programmed by parents who lived through the Depression to 'worry first and ask questions later.'"

Together, they kept one another on track. When well-meaning friends and family members pitied Danny's situation and said, "It's really terrible out there in the job market," he would gently respond, "We don't choose to believe that."

Danny and Melissa truly accepted and grieved the loss, but they also firmly rejected believing in a world of poverty and lack. Instead, they affirmed:

The Universe is lavish and abundant.

Danny felt the grief and confronted the pain with grace and courage. The fear and panic had subsided significantly as he opened himself up to new opportunities, and they came to him easily. Within two weeks of his job ending, he was offered a contract position that eventually led to a permanent job with an established company.

One of the lines we often hear when we lose a job is, *It's not personal,* which means that it's not personal to the employer. But of course to you as the employee, it's absolutely personal. It's haunting to believe that you were of great value to your company, yet now, in a very real way, they've said they can do the job without you. No wonder people are so often left feeling valueless.

When you feel that a work situation has indeed become personal, remember that it's your job to personalize the healing. How about telling yourself:

I am of value.

Remember to affirm that statement solely based on who you are, not because of what you do. Keep this in mind, too:

My value lies beyond any job.

Acceptance—that is, making peace with the reality that what just happened really has happened—can be the hardest part of dealing with job loss. You can't change what happened, but you can accept and grieve it in a positive, productive manner.

Many people believe that acceptance means liking what has happened or being okay with it. What it actually means, however, is that you acknowledge the reality that the loss has occurred. You have moved from the "shouldn't have happened" stage (denial), to the "it did happen" stage (acceptance).

In some ways, job loss is like a sudden death. It may feel like a betrayal. Similar to other losses we've discussed, one of the keys is to pay attention to what your mind is saying. If it's telling you, *I'm no one anymore. I don't matter in the world. I'm no longer relevant or of use to anyone,* these are negative beliefs that should not be repeated. You need to accept the reality of the loss, but not these negative beliefs. Ultimately, you must realize that what has happened is actually for your highest good. To get in touch with what lies beyond your sight, try the following affirmation:

Everything is unfolding for my highest good.

Accepting Your Authentic Self

When you are practicing acceptance in your surroundings and the world itself, you must also turn your focus inward and be willing to accept your authentic self. Be open to releasing and healing certain aspects or ideals you've been trying to hold yourself to, as well as expectations others have placed on you, but that don't serve you.

Kenneth was reflecting on his experience of love. He thought that whenever you really loved someone, your heart would eventually become bruised. He knew that most people aren't taught how to love in relationships, especially if they're gay.

In the past, gay men and women haven't had many open role models. When we see images of gay pride or individuals talking about being proud and comfortable in their skin, it can be tough to remember that such pride comes after years of feeling less than whole.

As Kenneth said, "I have quite a few scars on my heart, which come from being insecure about who I was and being ashamed of whom I loved."

Kenneth had spent years trying to be the person his parents wanted him to be, yet he longed to uncover his authentic self. Some gay people have a bigger challenge in this area due to extreme pressure from family members and society demanding that they be a certain way. Many don't often realize that some gay men and women have to grieve the mold that they were "supposed" to fit into.

Despite Kenneth's best efforts, he couldn't be the person his parents wanted him to be. And since he lacked good role models, he had a string of relationships in his 20s and 30s that were all imbalanced. His partners loved him, but he didn't love them back. Or he loved them deeply, and they didn't return the affection. He also had many long-distance relationships and now realizes that they were just another way of avoiding true intimacy. If someone were geographically distant, he wouldn't have to be a real participant in the relationship and be vulnerable.

All of this resulted in one wound after another. Then in his early 40s, Kenneth began working with a therapist. During one session, he was feeling particularly heartbroken about Gerry, a man he was dating, because once again, his feelings weren't being reciprocated. His therapist suggested that Kenneth try drawing what he was feeling.

Draw what I'm feeling? What would that look like? Kenneth thought to himself. He decided to open his mind and go for it. The first thing he drew was his heart, which was broken. It was a full heart, yet it had a crevice here and a big crack on one side. In another place, a chunk was gone, and on the bottom, it was completely shattered. He cried when he saw all the pain and grief.

When Kenneth showed the drawing to his therapist, she pointed to one area and asked, "What is this gash about?" She then requested that he write down what each crack represented, who had hurt him, and how it had happened.

It was an intense exercise, as he saw a grieving, wounded, depleted, dehydrated heart that had not received enough love. "I need more love," he said.

The therapist pointed out that while the issues seemed to him like they were only about being gay, they were actually about his lack of self-love and not having the willingness to be vulnerable in a relationship. He might have had these same issues had he been straight.

As Kenneth continued to work on it with his therapist, he came to realize that just speaking about his grief was filling in the cracks. "I was healing my heart through compassion toward those past experiences and finding appreciation for all that I had been through."

The more he talked and cried, the more vibrant the drawings of his heart began to look. It was taking on a new texture; the cracks and lines were filling in and becoming life affirming. Kenneth felt connected to the place where his spirit lived and learned that his heart could constantly regenerate itself. He relaxed into that knowledge and said:

Spirit lives unchanged and whole in
my beautifully worn, cracked, full heart.

Kenneth's release and grief over a false belief that he would never find a partner who loved him was healing. He now believed that he would love many people in his life, so why not spend some time in a relationship with himself, loving and treating himself like the partner he wished he had? He affirmed the following:

I am in a whole and loving relationship with myself.

Whether he was going on a fun hike by himself, getting a massage, or buying himself flowers, he relaxed into being in a really good relationship with himself. "I became more understanding and forgiving," he said, "and that's how I looked at it. I knew that if I was ever going to have a relationship with a partner who was loving, I had to create it within myself first."

Kenneth eventually did find that relationship with Dan, and to this day he repeats his favorite affirmations over and over:

I am living a balanced life.

In my relationship, I am giving and receiving love.

Today, Kenneth is risking more although he still has plenty of lessons and pattern breaking to do. For example, he told Dan early on, "I'm gonna break your heart."

A bit stunned, Dan asked, "What do you mean?"

"When two people are in love," Kenneth said, "they ultimately break each other's hearts."

"I don't choose that reality," Dan said. "I believe that if we're in love, we're going to break each other's hearts *wide open.* Love will crack open those closed, shutdown places in our hearts."

Kenneth didn't expect that response and had never seen it in that way. It made him realize that he was still engaged in negative thinking—this discovery was one of the many gifts the relationship gave him. He got to see things differently and shine a light on some of his issues. His partner's response was a reflection not of the wound, but of the opening that can be created: a more loving view and positive belief about love. Their relationship remains strong, and they continue to open and heal each other's hearts.

Kenneth's issues were around his identity and lack of self-love, but many people have grieved over the loss of who they thought they should be. Some men will grieve the six-pack abdomen they hoped they might achieve, and many women will have to let go of that "bikini body" they'll never attain. Others wish they were taller, shorter, or even another race. In the end, we all must grieve these "wish we were" thoughts and move toward happiness and acceptance as our true reality.

Let's take a little more time to examine this type of grief.

Grieving What Never Was

Most of us understand how we feel about the people and pets we've lost—but there are other kinds of grief, of course, including the type we feel regarding our assumptive lives. The following is a perfect example.

Dawn had done a lot of work on healing her cancer. Her journey had included Western medicine as well as complementary treatments. She now sat in a support group and shared that she was cancer-free, but still overwhelmed with sadness. "The news about my cancer treatment is good, so why do I feel so sad?" she asked.

While she had done her healing work, she hadn't taken the time to grieve. What did she need to grieve with cancer? Many things. The completely cancer-free life that she had expected turned out not to be a reality. Dawn needed to express her sadness about that loss. A couple of helpful affirmations would be:

I fully allow myself to be sad.

All experiences make me stronger.

Some people with cancer find it helpful to repeat healing affirmations along with affirmations about grief. The "normal" they knew is gone forever, but they can find a new normal:

I honor the loss of the life I thought I was going to have, and I embrace the new life ahead of me.

Dawn, like so many of us, believed that her body was invincible and nothing bad would ever happen to her, yet illness had come to her door. Her affirmation could be:

I am responsible for my health, but I am not to blame for my illness.

YOU CAN HEAL YOUR HEART

She was angry because she believed her body would warn her before something bad happened. It didn't, so she needed to forgive her body for "betraying" her:

I forgive my body.

I love my body.

Releasing Unhealthy, Unrealistic Ideals

Grief can also come from your picture of the ideal mate you thought you would find. You may have been so focused on waiting for Mr. or Mrs. Right to share your life that you woke up one day and realized that most of your life had in fact passed you by. That can lead to sadness and depression, the source of which is hard to identify. You don't realize that your depression is a form of grief. You have to mourn for the person who didn't show up and the life that never was. The good news is that when you take the time to grieve that loss—maybe for the first time in your life—you can finally live fully in the moment.

Deirdre, who attended a workshop on healing grief, said, "When I finally identified what I was feeling, I was overcome with tears. There was such a sadness that 'he' didn't show up. But a great relief followed the tears when I realized that my search was over. The rest of my life could be about me."

Your perfect mate may or may not show up, but it doesn't matter because there is a newfound freedom that comes with accepting reality and living your life fully for yourself.

Another type of grief you may need to work through is the career success you hoped for but never achieved. You believed you were supposed to be a famous dancer, a Pulitzer Prize–winning author, or a movie star . . . but it never happened. Of course this feels like bad news, but you have to accept your destiny and appreciate your life. You can spend your time being upset that your big break hasn't happened (which will provide you with a day-to-day experience of misery), or you can realize that your career is just one more expression of yourself, and you can dance, whether or not you have a huge audience. You can enjoy writing, even if it's only for your writing group. You can act for the joy of it, even if you don't have an Academy Award on your mantel.

When you watch a movie and the plot takes an unexpected twist, you don't get up and start yelling at the movie screen that it isn't following the story line you envisioned. It's the same with your unseen grief. Your life is like a movie with a plot that is constantly unfolding and is beyond your control. Just as you wouldn't stand up in the middle of the theater shaking your fist at the screen, don't stand up in the middle of your life and blindly shout at the things that are unfolding. Feel them, grieve them if they are losses, and don't add negativity to the mix. You will find that grief has a wondrous power to heal and give comfort to all your losses.

❧ ❧ ❧

Just as there are many different types of connections and attachments, there are many different types of losses. As you begin to recognize the loss as real, then and only then can you begin the healing process. In this chapter, we've covered a variety of seen and unseen losses, yet you may be able to think of others we haven't mentioned. Regardless of the type of loss, it always deserves its due.

All of my losses deserve healing.

Grief will heal all my losses.

Whether your loss was something that happened in the external world or was an expectation of a life that didn't turn out in the way that you expected, healing is always possible. The unseen gift is that when you fully feel and heal your grief and let go of your expectations, you'll find yourself, for the first time, truly living in the present moment.

∼

CHAPTER SEVEN

YOU CAN HEAL YOUR **HEART**

This final chapter is a reminder that life is always moving toward healing. We each carry underdeveloped parts of ourselves that long to be acknowledged and healed. They may show up as judgments, betrayals, breakups, or one of a million other challenges that we face.

Healing needs only your openness and willingness, because life loves you. If you're open to unlocking any insights when you experience a loss, you are on the right path. And if you're not, life will still bring you the lessons you need to find healing. Although you may misinterpret these lessons as a type of punishment, they are just part of the experiences of life.

Letting Go of Judgment and Resentment

Penny had been in Hollywood for three years, and she was sure she was going to be somebody. She had come from a small town in Iowa and had moved to California to study acting when she was 23. She'd gotten small parts here and there, but was mostly waiting for her big break.

Her friend Cindy had gotten her a job catering. It was perfect because if a big part came along, she wouldn't have to quit a job, or if she did a commercial workshop, she could just take a week off. Catering also allowed her to do something she never expected: glimpse into other people's lives. She even catered for some movie stars, and always had a story on hand about how she and Cindy worked an event for Elizabeth Taylor and how nice Elizabeth was to everyone. Cindy made the decision that when she became famous, she would similarly make an effort to be kind to everyone she met.

Catering also led her to work for some millionaires and even some billionaires. One night, Penny and Cindy were catering for a family called the Grossmans. She didn't know how they had made their money, but it clearly wasn't through acting or any other artistic talent.

They had a waterfall in their living room that was large enough for a plane to land in, and there were more bedrooms and bathrooms than she could count. Cindy said, "The artwork here is worth more than you and I will ever make in our whole lives." But Penny found the opulence off-putting. She made negative comments all night and was glad when the gig was over.

When Penny landed a part as a waitress on a popular sitcom, she was ecstatic. She had two lines ("What would you like for lunch? The chef salad is great!") and practiced them for days. She said them seriously, lightheartedly, and even tried a Southern accent.

The part went fine, but her two lines as a waitress didn't equal a career. For the next ten years, she played the neighbor, the salesclerk, the waitress, and the maid. All the while, catering remained a stable way to support herself. Cindy, her friend, had left catering and acting to go into real estate, but they remained good friends.

As Penny was getting older, she was competing with younger women for roles and felt that larger breasts might give her an edge, so she started saving money to get a breast enlargement. She saw a recommended doctor, and the first thing he did was give her a breast exam. He was speaking to her in a soothing, encouraging voice that suddenly turned serious.

"Did you know that you have a lump?" he inquired. "Feel this. How long has it been there?"

Penny was stunned as she felt it. "I have no idea," she said. "I don't know why I didn't notice it."

"That's why lumps can be so dangerous—they can be hard to spot."

When he told her that she needed to see an oncologist, Penny told him that she didn't have health insurance.

"Call for an appointment anyway," he said, "and let them know that. They have a lot of programs available to help you afford it."

When she called and told the receptionist that she had no insurance, she was told that on every Tuesday, the doctor saw patients at the Grossman clinic.

Penny was relieved to find out at the clinic that they had a number of programs that would help cover her costs. But then came the devastating news that she had cancer and needed to have a mastectomy. She was relieved when she learned that all of these costs would also be covered by the same cancer foundation.

Although the practicalities would be handled, Penny fell into a deep depression that persisted for some time. Even when she found out that the foundation would also pay for breast reconstruction, Penny couldn't find a way out of her melancholy. She realized what many people with cancer come to understand: You must grieve for the life you knew that is now over. You will never again have a cancer-free existence. You will have a different life—one you weren't expecting, but it can still be a wonderful life.

Many of us often forget to take the time to mourn this type of loss. For some, it's the loss of innocence or the loss of their health. For others, it may be the realization that bad things can and do happen. Penny, like so many individuals, learned that she would have a long life, but she had to do the grief work.

A day after the surgery, Penny's yoga instructor came to visit her at the cancer center and talk to her about some of these concepts. She said, "Penny, you want to grieve fully for the life that was and embrace the new life that will come. This can be an important time of transition, and you should let go of resentments, low-level thoughts, and judgments. Try to forgive and enter your new life clean."

"I don't have a lot of judgments and resentments."

The yoga instructor wisely replied, "That's perfect. Telling the Universe that you have no judgments or resentments will invite any of those you may have to come to the surface to be healed. Good for you for being willing."

Penny later wondered what kind of judgments she had and what kind of lessons she needed to learn. The next day, Cindy came to pick her up from the cancer center and help get her settled at home. As she puttered around the room, packing up her friend's things, she said, "Isn't it ironic that the Grossmans—the family you so hated—ended up creating the foundation and clinic that saved your life?"

Penny was startled. She hadn't put the billionaire family together with the cancer center. "Oh my gosh, Cindy! How did I not make the connection? My younger self never considered whether they gave money to charity or shared their wealth in some way. I realize that I gave movie stars a pass and judged everyone else."

This was truly a new beginning for Penny, as many things like this unfolded that needed to be healed.

We often forget that grief is a way we manage change. And illness always represents change. Some powerful affirmations would be:

There is unseen goodness in the world.

I receive all the lessons that life has in store for me.

Finding the Meaning after Loss

As we've previously discussed, Elisabeth Kübler-Ross identified the Five Stages of Grief: *denial, anger, bargaining, depression,* and *acceptance.* And later it was thought that there may also be a sixth stage—*finding meaning after acceptance.* Sometimes when we feel our grief fully, we can find profound meaning along with the healing.

Gail Bowden's story comes to mind because one of her children, Branden, was born with spina bifida, but Gail was determined to give him a wonderful life. Branden grew up a very happy child. He loved the color yellow, and later on, developed such a passion for Volkswagen Beetles that he amassed a toy collection of the cars.

When he was 17, Gail walked into his room one day and found him unresponsive. He was immediately transported to the hospital, and Gail sat with the doctor who gave her the sad news that her son would never wake up again. She asked if they were certain. Then she asked the nurse for a pen and wrote: "When the time comes, we will donate his organs." The nurse read the note and looked at Gail. She took her hand and told her that they didn't have to talk about that now, but Gail replied, "I may never be able to say those words, but I want you to make that happen for me."

Gail thought, *I can't believe that this is actually happening, but if they can't save his life, then Branden should get to save other lives.* She went to the operating room with Branden where they extubated him (took him off of life support), and she sang "Amazing Grace" as she waited for his heart to stop. Gail did her best to deal with the loss and remain optimistic and hopeful about the future. There were days when the sun's rays shone so brightly that one of Branden's friends from school told her that when the sun is shining, he knows that it's Branden smiling down on them.

A few years later, Gail and her other son, Bryan, moved into a new apartment, right before he went to boot camp. Gail sat unpacking boxes when she heard a knock at the door. She had arranged in the next week for a company to send someone over to paint the apartment yellow, and the man at the door explained that he was Ken, the painter.

"You're a week early," Gail told him.

"A job in the area was canceled, so the company sent me over," Ken replied.

"Well," said Gail, "everything is still in boxes. I wanted to organize things before you came, but since you're here, you might as well go ahead and start."

Ken began painting, and while Gail continued to unpack, he asked her if she lived there alone. She said, "My son, Bryan, is in boot camp. He joined the Air National Guard Reserves."

"Do you have anyone to keep you company while he's gone? Do you have any other kids?"

Gail had dealt with the awkwardness of that question before. Sometimes she would go into the whole story of Branden, but other times, she might answer, "It's just Bryan and me." This time, however, the question caught her off guard. She stood there, startled, thinking about what to say. She simply said, "I had another son named Branden who died when he was 17."

"I'm so stupid," Ken replied. "I always stick my foot in my mouth. So sorry for asking."

"That's okay," she told him, and he continued to paint. Then, after a few minutes, Ken said, "I'm sorry about your son. I know what it's like to be very sick. I was on dialysis and almost died four years ago, but my life was saved by a kidney transplant."

"When did you have your transplant?"

"In 2008," replied Ken.

"When in 2008?"

"February."

"February what?"

"February 13th" he said. "I'll never forget the date."

"Branden died on February 12th."

"Oh, no, it's not the same," Ken quickly said. "My donor was a 21-year-old who died in a car accident."

"Oh," said Gail, as she went back to packing and Ken went back to painting.

After a little while, Gail needed to run an errand, and she left Ken alone in her apartment with one wall painted yellow. When she returned, she found him standing right where she had left him. He hadn't made any progress.

"Is there something wrong?" Gail asked.

"I lied to you."

"You're not a painter?"

"No, not about that. I do have Branden's kidney."

"What?"

"When you told me that Branden was your son's name and you were Gail, I immediately realized that I'd received a note from you after I had the transplant. I was given the option to write back to you, and I'm so ashamed that I never did."

Gail, stunned, immediately picked up the phone and called the transplant center. She reached her counselor and said, "I hired a painter, and he tells me that he has Branden's kidney. How can we be sure?"

He said, "Wow, the odds of that occurring would be almost impossible, but give me his name."

Gail asked Ken his full name and gave it to the counselor. He opened up the confidential file and realized that indeed, Ken had received one of Branden's kidneys. Gail began to cry, and the painter said, "I do have his kidney, don't I?"

When Bryan called home from boot camp and heard what had happened, he said, "Mom, it's like Branden came home."

This story is a great example of how the Universe can work. We deeply believe in the affirmation *Life loves us,* although you may wonder how that applies in loss. As we mentioned, it doesn't mean that you won't experience loss—but depending on how you hold, perceive, and think about that loss, life can be there for you, even cradling you through your toughest times.

In the midst of Gail's loss, for instance, she accepted the tragedy that was in front of her but was determined that Branden would live on. How many of us say that when our loved ones die, they will continue on? We must remember that life cannot die; souls cannot die; and in Branden's case, some of his physical body wouldn't die. Gail was determined for Branden to live on by saving the lives of others. Two people can see because of Branden, and eight people have increased mobility and less pain because of Branden's tissues. This is especially powerful for Gail because Branden was in a wheelchair his entire life!

Later on, when Gail met Ken's wife and kids, she realized how much his children had needed him when Ken thought he was dying. She was gratified when she came face-to-face with a family that had been in such dire straits and overcame it. Not only had Ken's life been saved, but his wife and kids' lives had also been dramatically impacted.

You may think, *Well, Gail probably lived in a small town, and it was a coincidence that Ken ended up as her painter.* But consider these facts: Gail might have painted the room herself and never met Ken, or Gail might have hired a different company. The painter might have come when he was actually scheduled, and Gail would have had all the boxes put away and not been present to talk to him.

You may still say, *Okay, so some coincidences may have just lined up.*

The reality is that Gail lives in Buffalo, New York, and there are 18,000 painters in the area! The odds of her choosing Ken were only .006 percent. Life can hand us unexpected gifts when we're open to them, even in loss.

Gail's acceptance of her loss helped her work through her grief and find profound meaning in Branden's life and death. Her healing journey helps determine how she will lead the rest of her life, as well as continue to honor her son's life.

* * *

Life has a meaning all its own. It often doesn't turn out the way you expected, but it has a rhythm unto itself. It is full of twists and turns that often disrupt your peace of mind. Life brings you changes and challenges that you never hoped to experience. Once you allow yourself to feel the pain of those changes, accept the loss, and work through the grief, you'll learn the truth about life: *No matter what happens to you, you <u>can</u> heal your heart.*

~

AFTERWORD

When people think of loss, the idea of finding meaning or anything beneficial from it seems contradictory. But whether it's a breakup, divorce, or even death, there *is* more to be found, depending on how you hold the thoughts around it. It's not that you can stop the loss from occurring; it's that your thoughts change everything that comes after the loss.

Grief is a matter of the heart and soul. Grieve your loss, allow it in, and spend time with it. Suffering is the optional part. Remember that you come into this world in the middle of the movie, and you leave in the middle; and so do the people you love. But love never dies, and spirit knows no loss.

Since your thinking shapes the experience of your loss, why not make your intention to have a tender, loving experience of grief? And keep in mind that a broken heart is an open heart.

Let your thinking manifest hope to your sorrow. Choose your thoughts wisely. Be kind to yourself, and reflect on the loss with love. If you're grieving the death of a loved one, remember how you loved them when they were present; know that you can continue loving them in their absence. You *can* go from grief to peace.

Endings are also beginnings. We encourage you to use the affirmations and teachings throughout the book not only while working through a loss, but also in every aspect of your life. Pay attention to your thinking, and change it in areas that you don't have peace. By doing so, you'll bring more happiness into your life and to those around you.

Hard times can serve as a reminder that our relationships are a gift. Loss can remind us that life itself is a gift.

And don't forget to love yourself. You deserve it. *You* are a gift.

I love life, and life loves me.

I have lived and loved.

I am healed.

ACKNOWLEDGMENTS

Our heartfelt gratitude goes to all of the men and women over the years who have shared their lives with us at lectures and talks, and through countless e-mails and conversations. By opening up about their disappointments, losses, and grief, we can hopefully take those challenging and tender experiences to help others learn and grow.

Reid Tracy deserves special acknowledgment for shepherding this book. Thank you, Shannon Littrell, for your brilliant editing. And many thanks to all of our friends and colleagues at Hay House who have helped make this book all that it can be with their amazing dedication.

A book, like a person, needs a lot of support. Thank you to Erin Malone at WME; Andrea Cagan; Paul Denniston; Richard Kessler; David Kessler, Jr.; and India Williamson.

~

ABOUT THE AUTHORS

 **Louise Hay** is a metaphysical lecturer, teacher and bestselling author with more than 50 million books sold worldwide.

For more than 30 years, Louise has helped people throughout the world discover and implement the full potential of their own creative powers for personal growth and self-healing. Louise is the founder and chairman of Hay House, Inc., which disseminates books, CDs, DVDs and other products that contribute to the healing of the planet.

 **David Kessler** is one of the most well-known experts on grief and loss today. He co-authored two bestsellers with the legendary Elisabeth Kübler-Ross: *On Grief and Grieving* and *Life Lessons.* He is also the author of the bestselling hospice book *The Needs of the Dying*, which received praise from Mother Teresa; as well as *Visions, Trips and Crowded Rooms.* His services have been used by Elizabeth Taylor, Jamie Lee Curtis and Marianne Williamson when their loved ones faced life-challenging illnesses. In addition, David worked with the late actors Anthony Perkins and Michael Landon.

The founder of the cancer support group The Bogeyman in the Closet, he lectures on living life fully in the face of cancer. David has volunteered with the Red Cross, and he also serves on the board of the Farrah Fawcett Foundation.

www.louisehay.com
www.healyourlife.com
www.davidkessler.com
www.grief.com

Hay House Titles of Related Interest

YOU CAN HEAL YOUR LIFE, the movie,
starring Louise L. Hay & Friends
(available as a 1-DVD programme and an expanded 2-DVD set)
Watch the trailer at: www.LouiseHayMovie.com

THE SHIFT, the movie,
starring Dr Wayne W. Dyer
(available as a 1-DVD programme and an expanded 2-DVD set)
Watch the trailer at: www.DyerMovie.com

✿ ✿ ✿

STOP THE EXCUSES! How To Change Lifelong Thoughts,
by Dr Wayne W. Dyer

EXPERIENCE YOUR GOOD NOW!
Learning to Use Affirmations, by Louise L. Hay

HOW TO HEAL A GRIEVING HEART,
by Doreen Virtue and James Van Praagh

NURTURING HEALING LOVE: A Mother's Journey of Hope &
Forgiveness, by Scarlett Lewis, with Natasha Stoynoff

PEACE FROM BROKEN PIECES: How to Get Through
What You're Going Through, by Iyanla Vanzant

THE REAL RULES OF LIFE: Balancing Life's
Terms with Your Own, by Ken Druck, PhD

THE SOUL MIDWIVES' HANDBOOK: The Holistic and Spiritual
Care of the Dying, by Felicity Warner

THE TOP FIVE REGRETS OF THE DYING:
A Life Transformed by the Dearly Departing, by Bronnie Ware

All of the above are available at your local bookstore,
or may be ordered by contacting Hay House (see next page).

✿ ✿ ✿

We hope you enjoyed this Hay House book. If you'd like to receive our online catalogue featuring additional information on Hay House books and products, or if you'd like to find out more about the Hay Foundation, please contact:

Hay House UK, Ltd.,
Astley House, 33 Notting Hill Gate, London W11 3JQ
Phone: 0-20-3675-2450 • *Fax:* 0-20-3675-2451
www.hayhouse.co.uk • **www.hayfoundation.org**

❧ ❧ ❧

Published and distributed in the United States by:
Hay House, Inc., P.O. Box 5100, Carlsbad, CA 92018-5100
Phone: (760) 431-7695 or (800) 654-5126
Fax: (760) 431-6948 or (800) 650-5115
www.hayhouse.com

Published and distributed in Australia by:
Hay House Australia Pty. Ltd., 18/36 Ralph St., Alexandria NSW 2015
Phone: 612-9669-4299 • *Fax:* 612-9669-4144 • www.hayhouse.com.au

Published and distributed in the Republic of South Africa by:
Hay House SA (Pty), Ltd., P.O. Box 990, Witkoppen 2068
Phone/Fax: 27-11-467-8904 • www.hayhouse.co.za

Published in India by: Hay House Publishers India, Muskaan
Complex, Plot No. 3, B-2, Vasant Kunj, New Delhi 110 070 • *Phone:*
91-11-4176-1620 • *Fax:* 91-11-4176-1630 • www.hayhouse.co.in

Distributed in Canada by: Raincoast Books, 2440 Viking Way,
Richmond, B.C. V6V 1N2 • *Phone:* 1-800-663-5714
Fax: 1-800-563-3770 • www.raincoast.com

❧ ❧ ❧

Take Your Soul on a Vacation

Visit www.HealYourLife.com to regroup, recharge, and reconnect with your own magnificence. Featuring blogs, mind-body-spirit news, and life-changing wisdom from Louise Hay and friends.

Visit www.HealYourLife.com today!

YOU CAN HEAL *your* HEART

ALSO BY LOUISE L. HAY

BOOKS/KIT

All Is Well (with Mona Lisa Schulz, MD)
Colors & Numbers
Empowering Women
Everyday Positive Thinking
Experience Your Good Now! (book-with-CD)
A Garden of Thoughts: My Affirmation Journal
Gratitude: A Way of Life (Louise & Friends)
Heal Your Body
Heal Your Body A–Z
Heart Thoughts (also available in a gift edition)
I Can Do It® (book-with-CD)
Inner Wisdom
Letters to Louise
Life! Reflections on Your Journey
Love Your Body
Love Yourself, Heal Your Life Workbook
Meditations to Heal Your Life (also available in a gift edition)
Modern-Day Miracles (Louise & Friends)
The Power Is Within You
Power Thoughts
The Present Moment
The Times of Our Lives (Louise & Friends)
You Can Create an Exceptional Life (with Cheryl Richardson)
You Can Heal Your Life (also available in a gift edition)
You Can Heal Your Life Affirmation Kit
You Can Heal Your Life Companion Book

FOR CHILDREN

The Adventures of Lulu
I Think, I Am! (with Kristina Tracy)
Lulu and the Ant: A Message of Love
Lulu and the Dark: Conquering Fears
Lulu and Willy the Duck: Learning Mirror Work

CD PROGRAMMES

All Is Well (audio book)
Anger Releasing
Cancer
Change and Transition
Dissolving Barriers
Embracing Change
The Empowering Women Gift Collection
Feeling Fine Affirmations
Forgiveness/Loving the Inner Child
How to Love Yourself
Meditations for Personal Healing
Meditations to Heal Your Life (audio book)